THE
PASTORAL
SEARCH
JOURNEY

◆◆◆

THE
PASTORAL
SEARCH
JOURNEY

A Guide to Finding Your Next Pastor

◆ ◆ ◆

John Vonhof

THE
ALBAN
INSTITUTE
Herndon, Virginia
www.alban.org

The Alban Institute
2121 Cooperative Way, Suite 100
Herndon, VA 20171

Unless otherwise noted, all Scripture quotations are from the New Revised Standard Version of the Bible, copyright © 1989, Division of Christian Education of the National Council of the Churches of Christ in the United States of America, and are used by permission.

Cover Design by Spark Design.

Library of Congress Cataloging-in-Publication Data

Vonhof, John.
    The pastoral search journey : a guide to finding your next pastor / John Vonhof.
        p. cm.
    Includes bibliographical references (p. 167).
    ISBN 978-1-56699-402-6
    1. Pastoral search committees. 2. Clergy--Appointment, call, and election. I. Title.
    BV664.V64 2010
    254--dc22
                                2009050042

     10   11   12   13   14   VP   5   4   3   2   1

Contents

◆ ◆ ◆

*This book is dedicated to the men and women
who serve on pastoral search committees.*

Preface

Conducting a search for your church's next pastor is a serious task. Fortunately, those entrusted with this complex assignment do not make the journey alone. They can count on support from their church board and membership at every step. What else is necessary?

A lot, in fact. Many churches have not had to manage a pastoral search process for ten, fifteen, or even twenty years. Search committee members—typically board members and actively involved lay members—often do not understand the multitude of tasks that make up the search process. Could your congregation step up to the challenge?

This book was born in pastoral search committee meetings. As we struggled with the process in the mid-1990s, we learned much about what we did not want to do and about what we needed to do to be effective. We also often found ourselves in an undefined process in which we were on our own to choose what we did, how we did it, and in what order we did it. During our search I realized the need for a book about managing the pastoral search process. *The Alban Guide to Managing the Pastoral Search Process,* published in 1999, has helped thousands of congregations.

Now, by 2010, much has changed. We communicate differently. The Internet has redefined how we talk to one another and has given us access to information in ways we never thought possible. These changes can help a search committee. Committees now have more ways to inform others of their search and to connect with pastors. The committee has a greater ability to present its church in the best possible light through the congregation's website. For that reason, this revision is needed. Every chapter has been revised, with new material added. A new introduction takes the reader through the search journey, and new chapters discuss interim pastors and the use of the Internet. And finally, new appendixes provide pastoral search resources.

But for the moment, let's get back to our basic question. Could your board and church begin the search journey if your pastor announced today that he or she had accepted a call and would be leaving in two months? Could you manage the journey with the capable effort it deserves? These are only two of the questions that face search committees. To further complicate the process, the pool of available pastors is generally not large enough to satisfy the demand. What are committees to do?

The committee has a complex task before it. To have a clear focus, its process must be well thought out and free from unnecessary distractions. This book is designed as a guide to enable church boards to understand how to form a search committee, and then to help the newly formed committee understand the strategy and the order of its multitude of tasks. With a clear understanding of the journey, all will realize that it cannot be hurried.

Serving on a search committee requires a deep commitment to the Lord and to the local church. Much time and energy will be required before the task is completed. The process will likely take a minimum of six months and perhaps as long as two years. How the search journey is managed can make a difference in securing a good pastoral match, in minimizing the length of the search effort, and in reducing the stress on all parties. Whether your church is in a metropolitan area or in the countryside, whether yours is the only church of particular denomination in a large area, a congregation in an area with multiple churches of the same denomination, or an independent congregation, your search must be managed with high standards of excellence. We are not allowed the luxury of sitting back, placing a few ads, sending out a handful of letters, and then waiting for pastors to beat down our church door asking to serve as our pastor. We need to conduct a deliberate, well-thought-out search that treats both pastors and the process with respect.

We need to be competitive and thorough in our efforts. You may not regard the words *competitive* or *compete* as appropriate in talking about the pastoral search process, yet consider that when one church becomes vacant, it becomes simply one more in a large circle of churches without a pastor. Every congregation is working to find the pastor with the ministry skills that best match their gifts and needs. All are using the best resources they can develop. All are trying to present their church in the best light possible. Several may ultimately issue calls to the same pastor. Whether or not you like the words, the process is *competitive,* and churches do *compete* for pastors. Committees do not need to focus on this aspect of the process, but they should be aware of it. Each church begins its search with its own unique set of strengths and needs, and the pastors it considers have their own special ministry gifts and skills. Both the church and the pastor must be involved in a process that will create the best match for each.

This book is designed to allow people with little or no experience to serve effectively as members of a search committee. It is best if each committee member has his or her own copy of this book. All committee members should read through it at least once. While it provides detailed information to the committee chair, it also offers committee members an understanding of how the process is managed and why. The full committee will then understand what its task is and how its members can conduct a competent search. Although the book is written as a guide for those managing a pastoral search, it can also serve a search committee looking for other staff members.

Committees may use, modify, or skip over information, as appropriate to their situation. The letters, surveys, and questionnaires are given as examples to build on, not simply to copy. Make these your own. By adding and subtracting data, and by designing a format that you are comfortable with, you will create your own distinctive search materials and correspondence.

Throughout this guide, charts called *Task Clusters* illustrate the flow of tasks that are typically part of a search process. By following the arrows of the activities in these clusters, search committee members will be helped to think through the steps they need to consider, and to see them in the broader perspective of the whole picture. Review each task cluster after reading the chapter in which it is found and refer to the charts as you work step by step through the search process. If you are a "big picture" thinker, these task clusters will help you see the details of each chapter on one page.

As the search committee manages the process, denominational and regional requirements must be adhered to. It is the responsibility of the church board and its church counselor, minister supervisor, or other denominational liaison to help the search committee understand these requirements. However, this fact does not relieve the committee from its own responsibility of understanding them.

Denominations differ in their rules and procedures on how searches are conducted. Search committees in traditions where pastors are "called" will benefit the most from this book—whereas those in traditions where pastors are "sent" or "appointed" will find parts not applicable to their search efforts.

The text refers to both male and female pastors. If your church or denomination does not ordain women as pastors, substitute the masculine pronoun as appropriate. Names of people, churches, and cities used in this book are fictitious.

My prayers are with you as you seek God's will in the search for your next pastor.

I want to thank several people who are important to me. My wife, Kathie, was patient and supportive as I worked through the revision. Beth Ann Gaede, my editor at the Alban Institute, was again a joy to work with as she provided a wealth of positive feedback and constructive criticism that brought clarity to the manuscript. Jean Caffey Lyles, Alban's copyeditor, fine-tuned the manuscript with skill. The first version of this book in 1999 was good. This revision is even better, thanks to Beth and Jean. And finally, thanks to the staff of the Alban Institute for believing in this book.

Introduction

One might question whether there is a typical search for a new pastor. Indeed, if you have served on a search committee, you may have thought as you worked that you were inventing the process from scratch. Most churches have gone through the process many times. As one church fills its pastoral vacancy, another congregation loses its pastor and starts its own search. You are at a pivotal point in the life of your church. Understanding the journey is an important first step in starting the search process.

This journey has been going on for years. A previous pastor left, and your current pastor came and began ministry in your congregation. Many people in your church have known only the present clergy leader. He or she has been their pastor, preacher, counselor, teacher, leader, mentor, confidant, and perhaps friend. Members of your church have served with this pastor on committees and boards, as deacons and elders, as staff and associates. They have laughed and cried together, and have experienced God together.

Whether it has been five, ten, or twenty years, close relationships have developed. Some lay members have worked shoulder to shoulder with the pastor to advance the kingdom. For others the closeness is reflected simply in a kind word with a knowing handshake or a hug communicating that everything is fine. The pastor is their spiritual leader and they identify with him or her.

When your pastor announces that he or she is leaving, whether by retiring or by accepting a call to another church, closure is necessary. This pastor's period of ministry with your church is ending, and another ministry will begin. Church boards should acknowledge this change in pastoral leadership with special worship services, a potluck, an open house, or other celebration or recognition. Board members will focus on the termination with the current pastor. They will honor this pastor. They might help determine a ministry ending date, decide whether a parting gift will be given, plan the events to say good-bye, reassure the congregation that the board is in control, and of course support the pastor as he or she prepares to leave.

And now the road winds toward uncertainty. The period of vacancy and search will be trying to many. Some will leave your church; others will experience crisis and ask why God has taken away the pastor they had grown to love. Many will step up to make sure your church's ministry continues at its present level of excellence.

The church board must determine whether your denomination has policies about the formation of a search committee. Find out specifics, so that your search process will be conducted according to church policies. This is the first station on the journey (chapter 1). The second is the board's formation of the search committee, which now comes alongside the board and becomes active. The board focuses on caring for the congregation while the search committee makes sure that the church knows what is happening during the pastoral vacancy. Many boards wisely find an interim pastor to help manage the congregation as well as fill the pulpit. Chapters 2, 3, and 4 cover these important parts of a search process.

The third station on the journey is the point at which the committee takes steps to develop an accurate church profile. Through self-study, surveys, and discussions, committee members identify the congregation's strengths and weaknesses, its focus and direction, and the kind of leadership it needs in a pastor. They take this information and package it in ways that will capture the attention of interested pastors. This way station on the road is the key to getting the critical information that potential candidates will want to learn about your church. This important task cannot be rushed. It is explained in chapters 5 and 6.

The fourth section of the road is the search itself. This is usually the longest part. The word of your vacancy and search will spread. Buzz about the potential of your church will help influence those who see your website and hear about it through social-media sites and other channels. Names will be collected, letters and e-mails sent, phone calls made, references checked, and, at each step, impressions will be made. The field will ultimately narrow as some pastors drop out and others are added. Interviews will follow, and a select few will be invited to pay a visit to your church. Chapters 7, 8, and 9 cover this part of the search.

Now comes the fifth stage of the journey—the decision and call. Depending on your polity, this part may involve one or several pastors. It starts with the visits by the pastor or pastors selected at this point. They present their best side, and so does the congregation. The board, search committee, staff, and members all form opinions. The visiting pastors form opinions too. Meetings are held, votes are tallied, and a decision is reached. A letter of call is issued. This fifth stop on the search journey is explained in chapters 10, 11, and 12.

The sixth station on the search journey is a fork in the road. If the call is accepted, the road goes to planning for the installation of your new pastor. This task entails working out the details of the call's acceptance, making transition plans with the interim pastor and the new pastor, and working with the new pastor on planning for his or her family's move. This transition in covered in chapter 13. If, however, the call is declined, the road turns back and returns the search committee at least to the previous stage and perhaps further. The search resumes.

Some may think the sixth station is the end of the journey, but there is a final destination. The seventh stage is to manage a good start-up for the pastor and the congregation. The board, pastor, and staff work together to plan the church's ministry. This is an exciting time. God is good. He has directed the search efforts, and the hard work of the committee has paid off. Everyone's hope is that this stage will last for years and that the church will grow under the leadership of your new pastor. This too is explained in chapter 13.

Chapter 1

◆ ◆ ◆

The Pastoral Search Committee

A survey of pastors I conducted as I was preparing to write the first edition of this book indicated that every search process has room for improvement. The survey asked about the process, the picture the search committee presented, factors that influenced pastors' decisions, and what the search committee could have done better. Consider the following candid statements by pastors describing the search processes they have experienced:

- ◆ "The secretary did all the 'legwork' that resulted in an effort to call 'his kind of man,' which as it turned out, I was not."
- ◆ "I respected those making an effort to find a match for their vision more than those simply scrambling to fill the position."
- ◆ "Search committees should focus much more effort on the issues of leadership and followership—that is, seeking a pastor who is a leader and preparing their people for following."
- ◆ "Their search effort was poorly managed."
- ◆ "A search committee member who is enthusiastic about his or her church is hard to say 'No' to."

These comments hint at the impact the search process itself can have on potential candidates and suggest why your search committee will want to conduct a thoughtful and thorough search.

Before the Search Begins

The church board should make every effort to conduct an exit interview with the outgoing pastor. Your pastor has served, possibly for many years, and has valuable insights about your church. Use the interview process to discuss the pastor's thoughts on the church body, leadership, giving, member participation, and future directions. This interview can be conducted by several board members or by the entire board. If you have started the process of forming a search committee, include the committee chair.

If problem areas surface in the interview, commit time to resolving these issues. They could be problems related to leadership, vision and direction, lay involvement, or staff. If necessary, consider asking a judicatory leader, a consultant, or neighboring pastors for advice and help. Bringing in an interim pastor can also help the board resolve outstanding issues. Unresolved problems may also be detected by pastors who visit during the candidacy process, and those problems could negatively influence their interest in serving your church. Failing to deal with issues uncovered during the exit interview can exacerbate these problems when the new pastor arrives.

Beginning the Search

The board should call your congregation's denominational office to determine what is required in conducting a search. Regional or national organizations and leaders may have resources and publications to assist you, and they may have specific procedures that must be followed. These may pertain to the formation of the search committee, protocol for contacting pastors and obtaining lists of pastors interested in a call, formal letters of call, policies or recommendations about the use of an interim pastor, and guidelines for considering pastors from outside the denomination. This information should be passed on to the search committee.

If your denomination does not have guidelines for beginning a search, the question of when to begin may be open to debate. The incumbent pastor would often prefer the process to begin after she leaves.

She may believe that the questions and surveys about the congregation's gifts, needs, and future can wait. Some departing pastors indicate that beginning the search process before they leave does not allow proper closure for them, their family, and the congregation—and this is a realistic concern. Once a search has started, the congregation is focused on the search rather than on achieving closure and resolving issues. On the other hand, the board is concerned about the upcoming vacancy and would like to launch the process. Realizing that the post of pastor may be unfilled for anywhere from nine months to two years, boards will often agree that they must move quickly to form a search committee and get the process moving. Deciding when to start the process (and whether to conduct a congregational survey or ask for congregational input before the current pastor leaves) may be decided jointly by the board and the search committee.

The decision about when to start may also depend on whether the current pastor will be involved in the formation of the search committee. Some pastors are comfortable helping; others are not. Some denominations have rules about involvement of the outgoing pastor. The decision may also be based on the relationship between pastor and board, and between pastor and congregation. Talk candidly to your pastor. The decision on when to begin the search process is ultimately up to the board or the search committee.

Remember that you are moving from a relationship with your outgoing pastor into a new relationship with another pastor. The strengths and integrity of your former period of ministry should be the starting point for the new relationship. If you can work at making this happen, the relationship with your new pastor should grow in a positive direction. Consider arranging for the board and search committee to meet together and talk about the positive aspects of the church's ministry under the outgoing pastor. They could also meet with the pastor and discuss what has worked well over his or her tenure.

Formation of the Pastoral Search Committee

The pastoral search committee, or call committee, has a tremendously complex task—but one that can bring many rewards. Before discussing the makeup of the search committee, consider several important perspectives about this group. A search committee is given the task of finding the person God would have lead the congregation as its pastor. It could be said that your committee needs individuals who are both "head smart" and "heart feeling." For that reason, committee members should rank high in five areas: spiritual maturity and sensitivity, ability to work well in a committee setting, listening and communication skills, discernment, and involvement in the ministries of the church. An understanding of leadership and administrative skills is also helpful. The search team should also understand the church's vision and mission. While search committee members will be at different levels in the five areas, all must have an enthusiasm for their task that will carry them through the long process ahead.

As the board considers people for the committee, it needs to select members who are respected, have the time to commit, work well in a group, and are known to keep commitments and assignments. The committee should be made up of people who will accept the challenges of serving in this vital role and who exhibit a high level of commitment coupled with the essential skills.

Whether the search committee is chosen by the board or selected by a nominating committee or the congregation, the same considerations should be given to committee leadership, congregational representation, and size.

Committee Leadership

The search committee needs a strong leader to serve as chair. This person should be comfortable leading in a committee setting; have gifts and skills in organizing, administration, encouragement, and stating consensus; and be at ease speaking to groups. Strong secretarial support is also needed. The amount of paperwork generated by and tracked by a secretary can be overwhelming to anyone unfamiliar with handling agendas, minutes, letters, e-mails, and phone calls to multiple people—all at the same time. In choosing members for the committee, the board members should decide whether they will select people they want to serve as chair and secretary, and approach these two individually, or allow the committee members to choose their own leaders. There may be occasions when the chair and secretary share duties, and this approach may be useful if people have qualms about their ability or time to serve, or if the church is small. If you have rules in your bylaws or denominational policies about who may serve in these positions, follow those guidelines.

Congregational Representation

It is crucial that the search committee be made up of a cross-section of the congregation's membership. As you consider individuals, think about who can represent your congregation's various constituencies. A good balance of male and female members and of older and younger members is needed. You should not, however, compromise having qualified members who fit the five areas above simply to have all constituencies represented. If your church has specialized ministries, consider whether they should be represented too. Try to have at least one member who is also on the church board. This person should represent the board to the search committee and the search committee to the board.

Committee Size

The committee does not have to be large. Six to eight members is optimum. Some churches base the size of the committee on the size of the congregation. Larger committees can be unwieldy because not everyone will be able to attend every meeting, and some will be less intimately involved than others with minutes and action items. As you consider committee size, remember the pros and cons of having a smaller or larger group.

With more than eight on a search committee:

- ◆ *Pros:* You may gain a larger cross-section of the congregation, the skills helpful to run an effective search, and people to share in the tasks.

◆ *Cons:* Discussions, conference calls, and decisions become more difficult to manage; the meetings will have to be carefully structured and may last longer; and not everyone may be able to attend all meetings. In addition, the larger the group, the more likely it is that confidential information will leak.

With eight or fewer on a search committee:

◆ *Pros:* Discussions, conference calls, and decisions can be better managed; meetings can be less structured; and greater intimacy is possible.

◆ *Cons:* More work will have to be done by fewer people; less of a cross-section of the congregation may be represented; and some skills may be less available.

Approaching Prospective Committee Members

Preferably, the board selects those asked to serve. If your bylaws or church order requires a congregational vote to approve search committee members, follow those requirements. A letter similar to the sample below should be sent by the board secretary to all those being asked to serve, explaining in each case why they are being asked, and identifying the task. Modify the letter to meet your specific situation.

◆ ◆ ◆

The Anytown Community Church board took action last night to approve the formation of a pastoral search committee to manage the search for a new pastor. We also approved a list of people to serve on this committee. Individuals were approved on the basis of their perceived gifts and the unique perspectives they would bring to create a well-rounded committee. We would like you to be a part of this committee. If you agree to serve on this committee, you will be entrusted with a great responsibility. We have confidence in you and believe you would be a valuable member of our search team.

You are asked to reflect on the requirements to serve in this capacity, since the committee members must work intimately together. Our expectations of all committee members are:

- ◆ To be in constant prayer for Anytown Community Church and the search process.
- ◆ To be faithful in attending Anytown Community Church and its functions.
- ◆ To be familiar with Anytown Community Church's strengths and weaknesses.
- ◆ To be willing and able to take the time needed to prepare for meetings.
- ◆ To be committed to attending the committee's meetings.
- ◆ To respect confidences.

Our prayer is that you will consider this request in two ways. First, commit yourself to prayer to know God's will, and second, if you are married, discuss this request with your spouse, since serving will affect family life.

We anticipate that meetings will be held biweekly at the outset but could become more frequent as information flows in about available and interested pastors. Between meetings varying amounts of time will be required as work progresses, surveys are conducted, contacts are made, sermon tapes are received, and letters and e-mails are sent. We want you to understand the time commitment up front. Depending on your other church-related responsibilities, you may have to evaluate reducing those to allow for the time necessary to serve in this vital role. A search process typically takes between eight months and one year. However, it could extend beyond one year.

I am available to answer your questions about this responsibility. You are asked to respond to me no later than _____ [a date one week away]. Our prayers are with you as you consider your potential role in this important challenge to Anytown Community Church.

◆ ◆ ◆

Follow up the letter with a phone call to each prospective search committee member. Be sure you are sufficiently familiar with the search process to answer any questions. Stress that there are rewards in serving and that many individuals report a deepening of their faith as a result of serving on a search committee. The search process rewards those who serve as they become intimate with the life of their church, their denomination, the pastors they work with, and other search committee members. They will also experience a sense of accomplishment. Assure the search committee members that they will have the full support of the board and the congregation.

If the church has gone through a search within the past ten years, there may be church members who served on that search team. Consider arranging a meeting with former search committee members who can provide insights learned from their search.

Introducing the Committee to the Church

To keep the congregation informed about the search process, introduce the search committee during a Sunday worship service. The committee chair can say a few words about the committee and the process. At the same time, a brochure that includes photos of each search committee member with a brief biographical sketch and contact information can be distributed to members. The brochure might also briefly explain the search process and search committee covenant. Make the brochure available to members who are not present the day the committee is introduced, and put it on the church's website.

Committee Responsibilities

When the committee meets for the first time, the members should spend time getting to know one another. Hearing an account of the spiritual journey of each member will help the committee to bond. The first meeting is the perfect time to talk about commitment, prayer, trust, and confidentiality; a committee mandate; ground rules; a covenant; and a plan to manage the overwhelming amount of material a search generates. A mandate is the committee's assignment or task. Ground rules outline how the committee operates. A covenant is the glue that holds the committee together. Prayer and a commitment to confidentiality are especially critical to the committee's work.

Prayer

The committee must bathe the search process in prayer. From the beginning, prayer must be an integral part of the work, not simply something done at the start and close of meetings. You may choose to start meetings with a single prayer and close with conversational prayer. Respect those who may feel uncomfortable praying aloud; yet encourage them to join in when they become more comfortable doing so. This spiritual grounding through prayer is important for the search committee's cohesion.

The board and the congregation also need to pray regularly for the search committee and the search process. Include the committee's work in congregational prayers and in prayer requests during worship services. When there are specific immediate needs, activate your church's prayer chain. If you do not have a prayer chain, consider starting one to support the search committee. An e-mail list of church families allows a congregation to disseminate prayer requests and other information about the search (as well as other congregational news) to a large number of people with minimal effort. If your congregation does not have such a list, this would be a good time to create one.

The search committee must understand the role of prayer in discerning the Spirit's leading. Pause, reflect in silence, and pray before decisions are made, when the path is uncertain, when tensions build, and when praise is due. Each committee member must commit to pray daily for other committee members, for the search process, and for the pastors with whom the committee is in conversation. You will often feel the urge to hurry the process; focusing on prayer will properly ground you in the Spirit. God will honor your prayers for guidance.

Remember that for every pastor who begins ministry in a new congregation, another church loses its pastor. Another search committee will be formed and the whole search process repeated. Your success in finding the pastor to lead you is a loss for his or her former church. That church also needs to be remembered in your prayers. As you grieved when your pastor left, its members too will grieve. Consider writing a letter to that congregation's board and search committee after your new pastor arrives, letting them know that you are praying for them.

As your search committee considers pastors, you will become very close to some of these candidates, but you will select only one of them. Let those whom you do not select know that you will continue to pray for them as they continue their ministries. Some pastors will reevaluate their ministry after not getting a call and decide to stay put. Others will continue their search for a new church. Those pastors with whom you communicated for months, who shared deeply of themselves, but who did not receive a call from you, will appreciate your support. They all need your prayers.

Confidentiality

All members of the search committee must adhere to strict standards of confidentiality. Talk about this necessity at your first meeting. Define what it means for the members. What can they tell their spouses? What can they tell church members who ask about the search? Who speaks for the committee? The names of pastors being considered must be kept in confidence. When asking pastors to complete questionnaires or when conducting telephone or face-to-face interviews, state at the outset that confidentiality will be respected. Search committee materials, such as minutes with details about pastors, pastoral profiles, questionnaires, and notes from interviews, must all be kept confidential while the committee functions, and then properly disposed of when no longer needed. Confidentiality becomes more difficult as the search widens and the search committee tries to keep the congregation as well informed as possible, but it must be maintained for the sake of the search process and the pastors involved. Do your best to protect your church and pastors from rumors. Clarify with the board what it needs to know and what your authority and accountability will be for your committee's work.

Developing a Committee Mandate

It is wise to develop a mandate under which the search committee will operate. This mandate will provide the basis for all that the search committee does. Investigate whether your denomination has mandates for search committees. Some organizations may use the term *guidelines*. The board may provide input for the mandate or may leave it up to the search committee. Committee goals, procedures, and expenses might be covered. Items included in these areas might look like those below. Make your guidelines conform to any denominational guidelines for the search process.

1. The committee will conduct a search process that is to result in a prioritized list of pastors to be considered by the committee for a call to Anytown Community Church. The search committee will make recommendations to the board. The name or names will be submitted by the board to the congregation and a call extended to the pastor selected.

2. The committee will submit regular progress reports to the board and the congregation.

3. As part of the search process, the committee may prepare or arrange for qualified individuals or organizations to prepare the following materials:

    ◆ congregational questionnaire
    ◆ denominational church profile
    ◆ church information packet
    ◆ advertising
    ◆ pastoral search budget
    ◆ pastoral questionnaire
    ◆ procedures for interviews
    ◆ procedures for checking references
    ◆ procedures for personality and relationship testing
    ◆ compensation package
    ◆ pastoral job description or a definition of roles, responsibilities, and relationships
    ◆ other materials as required to carry out the committee's mandate
    ◆ search flowchart

4. The committee will determine evaluation and selection criteria.

5. The committee will define a process to present the nominated pastor or pastors for a congregational vote.

Setting Ground Rules

When first meeting as a committee, the group should consider establishing ground rules for the meetings and the process. These may concern committee functioning, support for one another, and the work of the committee. Possible ground rules include:

- ◆ Our search is founded on prayer.
- ◆ Members commit to pray daily for committee members and their work.
- ◆ We will meet in a member's home. (A home usually affords a warmer atmosphere than a room at the church—an enhancement to building community.)
- ◆ Meetings will begin and end at the scheduled times.
- ◆ Meetings will open with a devotional offered by one of the committee members.
- ◆ Members are responsible for completing tasks assigned to them by the agreed-upon due date.
- ◆ The chair manages the release of all information from the committee, unless otherwise determined.
- ◆ Decisions will be made by either majority vote or consensus. (Consider this guideline carefully. Requiring a consensus can be problematic, since one person can control the outcome. The committee might want to make decisions using another method.)
- ◆ Decisions about candidates will not be made until all information is received about all pastors being considered at a given stage of the process.
- ◆ The search committee will not rush the process.
- ◆ The committee will maintain close relationships and report to the board after each meeting.

Writing a Committee Covenant

It can be helpful for your search committee to have a covenant that all members agree to support. Members need to know that they can count on one another and that all are committed to the search. Areas of focus include prayer and commitment, accountability, and communications. It is good to share this covenant with the church body. It is good for members to know how committed the committee is to the search. Below is a sample covenant with sections on prayer and commitment, accountability, and communications.

◆ ◆ ◆

As members of the search committee for Anytown Community Church, we promise to abide by the following covenant:

PRAYER AND COMMITMENT

1. We pledge to pray daily for each member of the committee and his or her tasks.
2. We will pray to seek God's will for our entire church and its ministries, putting our individual perspectives aside.
3. We will pray daily for those pastors with whom we come in contact.
4. We commit to act with trust and integrity.
5. We specifically commit to maintain strict confidentially regarding all search discussions and correspondence.
6. We commit to conduct our search thoroughly.

ACCOUNTABILITY

1. We will be accountable to one another in a spirit of servanthood for tasks assigned to us.
2. We will be accountable to the board and the congregation and will seek God's will for the entire church body, rather than our individual wills.
3. We will recommend only a candidate whom we can support in a spirit of full unity.

COMMUNICATIONS

1. We will strive to be open with our ideas and feelings, in a spirit of honesty.
2. We will seek to communicate clearly and regularly to the board and congregation.
3. We will honor all pastors with whom we communicate.

◆ ◆ ◆

Meetings, Agendas, and Minutes

Initially, the search committee may choose to meet biweekly. However, when pastors are being interviewed and the search is narrowing, weekly meetings will be needed. When pastors are finally invited to visit the church and preach to the congregation (if allowed by denominational rules), special meetings may have to be scheduled. The visit will have to be reviewed, a decision made about the pastor just heard, plans made for the next visiting pastor, and pieces of the search puzzle fitted together to move toward a final selection.

Meeting agendas should be distributed in a timely manner. It is helpful for committee members to have agendas before a scheduled meeting so that they can plan and review material attached or previously distributed. The secretary may put together the agenda alone or with the chair. An agenda early in the search process will differ from one for a meeting after months of search and communication. Each new agenda needs to be built from the minutes of the previous meeting with thought given to new items or issues. Allow time for care and support of committee members as they become more intensely involved in the search process. Plan for a short time of worship at each meeting.

Minutes of all meetings should be distributed soon after the meeting so that committee members may review what they did and follow up on any actions they are responsible for before the next meeting. The minutes should be concise and complete. They serve as a summary of the search committee's actions and decisions and the matters heard, discussed, and decided about each pastor considered. Action items that require follow-through by committee members can be italicized for emphasis, with the assigned member's name noted. Another option is to put an "action items" column on the right side of the page—listing the person responsible and the due date for each item. Since it is helpful for the committee to see in the minutes the stage of consideration for a particular pastor, think about providing a sheet that shows all pastors being considered and where they are in the search process. Chapter 8, "Connecting with Pastors," includes an example of such a chart. Minutes should be given to the chair of the board, and any items that require board approval should be noted. Minutes may also be sent to the pastor acting as your counselor or supervisor, and to other individuals or committees with oversight responsibilities. Minutes are to be treated as confidential and should not be distributed to others or posted for the congregation to read.

An item easily overlooked is supplying each search committee member with an adequate binder and a suggested system of managing the flow of paperwork. Consider buying roomy three-hole binders for all members, with tabs for specific topics. Put copies of the committee's covenant, guidelines, and ground rules behind the first tab. Pastors' profiles should be filed alphabetically by last name. As pastors are discussed and profiles reviewed, all material and notes on a pastor should be filed with his or her profile. Decisions will be made at various points in the process. If the group decides to terminate communication with a pastor, members should remove his or her profile from their binders and store it apart from the active candidates' profiles. Possible tab headings:

- Committee Mandate, Ground Rules, and Covenant
- Agendas and Minutes
- Selection and Evaluation Criteria
- Congregational Questionnaire
- Church Profile
- Church Information Packet
- Pastoral Profiles
- Pastoral Questionnaire
- Hosting Visiting Pastors
- Congregational Updates
- Interim Pastor/Church Counselor/Supervisor
- Regional/Denominational Correspondence
- The Call Process and Call Letter

Committee Resources

Search committees should have current copies of their regional or denominational church directories and magazines. These publications are a good source of names and contacts useful in your search. If your denomination has a manual of church order or policies, a constitution, an official letter of call, and compensation guidelines, order copies. Some denominations have a packet of resources for search committees. Inquire about these resources at your regional or denominational offices. Familiarize yourself with any denominational materials that affect how your search committee may operate. Appendix A, "Pastoral Search Resources," lists websites and tools related to the pastoral search process.

Managing Search Expenses

Since most pastoral vacancies are unplanned, a church typically does not have a budget for its newly formed search committee. Several options exist, depending on how structured your budget and finances are. If you will not be paying a full-time interim minister, a simple method is to take the money normally budgeted for the pastor's salary and expenses and put it into a budget for pastoral search expenses. If you will be using an interim pastor, search expenses will need to be covered in some other way. One option is simply to charge expenses against an existing budget category. However, this method makes it harder to distinguish between search expenses and regular church expenses in that category.

Expense categories might include mailings, travel, telephone, testing, information packets, website development/updates, and miscellaneous items. Expenses for a part-time interim minister or guest pastors could be also charged to that budget. Remember that any candidate visiting your church needs to be reimbursed for all related expenses. Talk with your board about how to manage expenses. Typically, routine expenses would require committee approval, and receipts and invoices would be submitted to the church treasurer for payment. Determine what types of expenses require board approval, and set limits on how much can be spent without preapproval of the committee or board.

Avoiding Common
Search Committee Mistakes

Search committees commonly make ten mistakes that are important to avoid. Discussing these early on in the process will help keep the committee on track:

1. Making a decision based on first impressions. Take time to review a pastor's profile and materials thoroughly, and compare these with the selection and evaluation criteria.
2. Failing to conduct a complete and honest evaluation of your church to identify its strengths and weaknesses.
3. Choosing a pastor who is the exact opposite of, or exactly like, your former pastor.
4. Failing to look at the pastor's previous ministry terms for length, church size, and specialized programs started under his or her watch.
5. Choosing a pastor that the committee thinks the congregation members want rather than the one the church needs.
6. Selecting a pastor who may have a hard time adapting to the culture of your church, community, and locality. This anticipated difficulty may relate to church size, specialized ministries, rural or suburban context, big-city or small-town setting, or cross-cultural and ethnicity issues.
7. Failing to hold the search team accountable to its own ground rules—especially confidentiality.
8. Not holding all candidates to the same submission requirements. All candidates must submit the same materials (profile form, pastoral history, sermons, and so forth).
9. Allowing the board or certain members or groups in the church to "push" the process in a direction different from the one the committee might take otherwise.
10. Succumbing to pressure from committee members, the board, or members of the congregation to speed up the process.

Your Interim Pastor,
Church Counselor, or Supervisor

It is the duty of the pastor who is leaving to notify the regional or denominational offices that he or she will be leaving as of a certain date. If it falls in the regional leadership's area of responsibility, those officials will take the initiative and assign a judicatory staff member to your church. These individuals are selected and trained on the basis of leadership gifts and skills. Chapter 2, "The Interim Period," describes the benefits of using an interim pastor. Spend time understanding how an interim can help your board and congregation.

You may be assigned a counselor or supervisor to help your board and give assistance, if requested, to the search committee. These individuals are well versed in polity and denominational procedures.

The formation of the search committee is the important first step toward finding your next pastor. Make sure the committee understands that its responsibilities will pay dividends as the search progresses.

CHART 1.1 Task Cluster: The Pastoral Search Committee

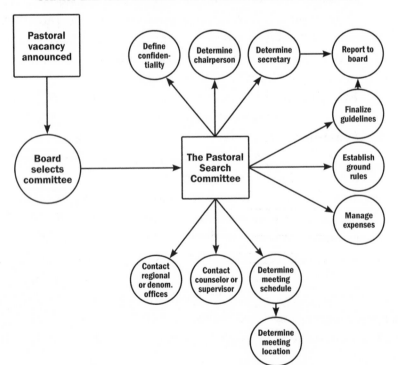

Chapter 2

◆ ◆ ◆

The Interim Period

The interim period, in simplest terms, is the time between pastors. This period is, however, far from simple. The church must continue to function. Worship needs to happen. The board must lead. The staff continues to work. Members must be taught and cared for. Visitors and new members must be introduced to the life of the church. It is here that an interim pastor fits into the plans of your congregation during the clergy leadership vacancy and the search process.

A congregation approaching an interval without a pastor has several options for pastoral support. Understanding these will help the board and the search committee determine their preference for ministry support.

- ◆ First, denominational or regional offices can help determine whether a trained interim pastor is available to serve your church.
- ◆ Second, retired pastors can be engaged to serve for a specific time period, perhaps until a new pastor is called.
- ◆ Third, the board can decide to use local pastors, or perhaps retired pastors, as weekly guest pastors. Using guest pastors for pulpit supply is discussed in chapter 4, "Managing the Congregation."

Interim pastors, sometimes called transition specialists, will provide the best support. They have been trained to help congregations end their relationships with previous pastors, conduct self-study and discern new directions, identify and develop new lay leaders, rethink denominational relationships, and build commitment to a new future. An interim pastor might be willing to commit from twelve to eighteen months of service. He or she may come to your church in a part-time or full-time role.

Long-term supply pastors are usually retired pastors who are able to work in the church for a specific length of time, perhaps from three to six months. These pastors usually provide only maintenance ministry—preaching, teaching, and pastoral care. They are typically not trained to do the work of an interim pastor.

Both interim and long-term supply pastors can provide the congregation with a sense of continuity that is not provided by weekly guest pastors, and both can support the search committee if there are procedural questions. They are often eager to visit with members and friends of the congregation. Both may be willing to attend board meetings to provide advice and support. Whether you use one or several interim pastors or long-term supply pastors, you will want to develop a contract that specifies the pastor's level of involvement with the board, committees, and member visitation, as well as whether he or she will serve part time or full time and for how long. Appendix A, "Pastoral Search Resources," lists several ministry websites available to help churches find an interim or supply pastor.

The Value of an Interim Pastor

The period your church is without a "settled" pastor (that is, permanent—or as permanent as any pastor can be) is crucial in the life of the church. An interim pastor can be invaluable to a congregation, performing whatever tasks are mutually agreed upon with the board. Leading worship and providing pastoral care will probably be high priorities. Even though members may not voice their concerns, they will wonder who will fill the pulpit and whether the preaching will be good, who will preside at funerals and weddings, who will baptize, who will call on the sick, who will provide counseling—all critical components of pastoral care. Members of the pastoral staff and other church employees may feel confused or anxious. Some individuals may have been wounded by the previous pastor or may be hurting over the loss of the pastor.

In addition to leading Sunday worship services and helping with pastoral care, the interim pastor can be a tremendous help to the board and search committee. The board may need help bringing closure to the former pastor's ministry; dealing with change; resolving issues of leadership, ministries, or structure; or addressing other issues left from the previous pastor's tenure. An evaluation of the church's ministries might be in order during this transition period. During the interim, the church's leaders and members may be under more stress than usual and can lose focus on their mission. An interim pastor can help with refocusing the church. The search committee might use an interim's assistance when determining how best to conduct a congregational self-study and develop a church profile. Other than that, interim pastors usually do not become involved with the search committee or process. With the help of an interim pastor, however, the church can emerge from the time between settled pastors stronger and with a renewed vision for its purpose and mission. This strength in turn helps the new pastor as he or she assumes leadership.

It is easy to think that your church does not need an interim pastor. However, the value an interim brings to the church board and the congregation cannot be underestimated. In some specific instances, an interim is highly recommended because healing is needed. Transitions will be harder:

- When the previous pastor served the congregation for ten years or more.
- When the pastor left because of conflict in the church body or leadership.
- When the pastor left in a storm of controversy surrounding some incident of pastoral misconduct.
- When specific unresolved issues are creating discord within the congregation.
- When the church is large.
- When the church has a large pastoral staff.

Most denominations have policies governing the use of interim pastors. One of these is that an interim cannot be a candidate to become a congregation's "permanent" pastor.

The Expense of an Interim Pastor

An interim pastor serving full time should be paid a salary and benefits comparable to the former pastor's. If the interim is serving part time, adjust the compensation accordingly. If you approach a retired pastor to serve your congregation as a long-term interim pastor, expect to pay a base salary, travel expenses to and from the church, and expenses for local mileage and hospitality, as well as to provide housing. In general, congregations find that the benefits of having an interim pastor easily justify the additional costs.

Regional or denominational offices may have guidelines for payment to pastors providing various levels of leadership, and the board should make use of their expertise in developing a contract. Items that should be considered include:

- ◆ Typical weekly duties.
- ◆ Expected hours per week.
- ◆ Length of service.
- ◆ Accountability.
- ◆ Responsibilities, such as:
    1. Assisting with closure of the former pastor's ministry.
    2. Planning and leading worship and preaching.
    3. Attending board meetings.
    4. Assisting the board with resolving any difficult issues affecting the congregation as a whole.
    5. Assisting in a congregational self-study.
    6. Working with the search committee to develop the church profile.
    7. Reviewing the church's ministries and structure.
    8. Advising the board on how to manage the "start-up" period when the new pastor arrives.
- ◆ Salary figure and payment schedule.

- Expense reimbursement policies and procedures.
- Benefits (health coverage, vacation time, days off).
- Policy that the interim cannot be considered as a candidate for the post of pastor.

The interim period is a challenge for the church. Ministries continue. Members and visitors come and go. Care is needed. The church board and staff have their hands full. Using an interim pastor can benefit the church during this period of uncertainty.

CHART 2.1. Task Cluster: The Interim Period

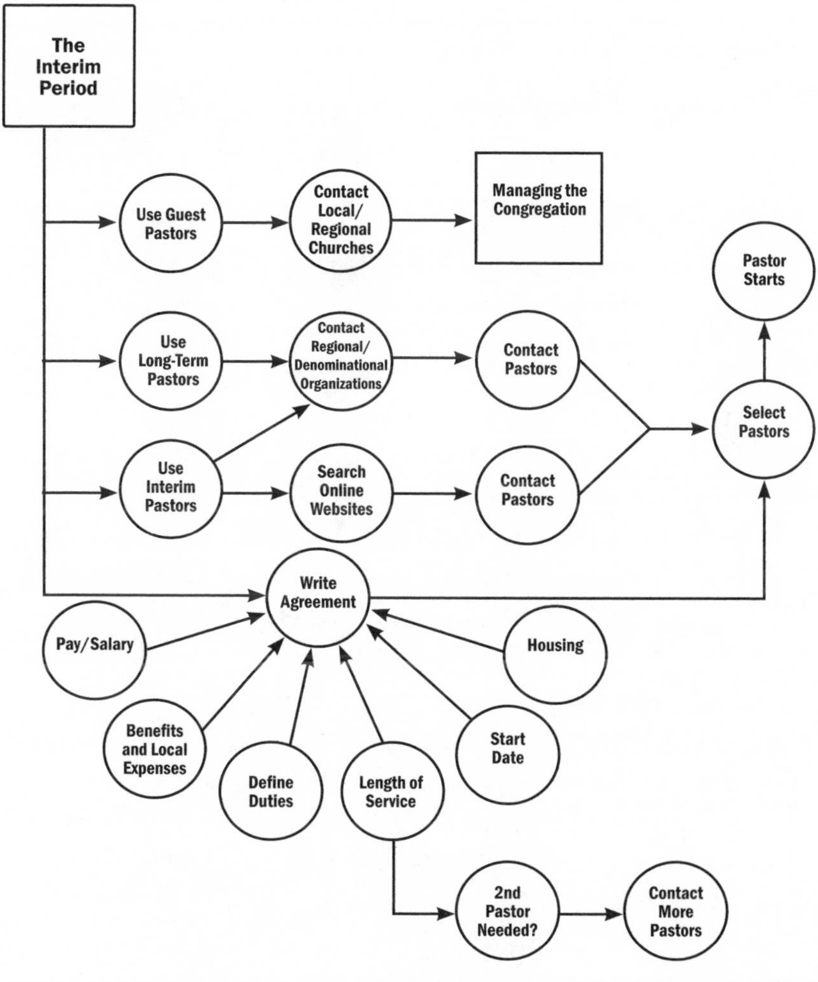

Chapter 3

◆ ◆ ◆

Using the Internet

In the ten years since the first edition of this book was published, we have seen tremendous changes in the way a church can spread the word about its pastoral search. The Internet and its capacities have surpassed our wildest imagination. People and companies worldwide are using the power of the Internet to spread the word about their products and services, and the church can do the same.

Almost everyone by now has heard of and used the Internet—typically referred to as "the Web." In fact, most of us cannot fathom how we managed before the Web. One of the most important things to remember about the Web is that people want information—that's what they search for. To understand how committees can use the Web, think first about the members of your church and what they want to know about the pastoral search process. They want to know that someone in leadership is concerned about the pastor's departure and the congregation's search for a new pastor. They want to know how long it will take, how the search will be conducted, who can answer questions, how members will get updates and how often, who will lead worship and teach, how the time between pastors will affect parishioners and the ministries of the church, and more. Second, think about the pastors with whom you come in contact during the search process—or those who find your website through a search engine or word of mouth. What do they want? They are looking for information about your church—its size, worship style, ministries, staffing and organization, beliefs, vision, and more. This chapter details how the search committee can use the power of the Web to give people the information they are looking for.

Your Church's Website

Many churches today have websites that extend their presence to a new arena called cyberspace that has worldwide reach. Some sites are simple, and others are complex. If your church has a website, it can be used to your advantage in your search. If your church does not have a website, you might talk to the board about creating one. The advantages are clear:

- ◆ Members can see program and ministry information.
- ◆ Potential visitors can find your church and learn about it.
- ◆ Ministry information can be made widely available.
- ◆ Sermons and devotionals can be shared.
- ◆ The community can learn about your congregation's people and work.

Creating a custom website can cost hundreds or even thousands of dollars, depending on the complexity of the site and who does the work. The monthly fees to host the site are relatively inexpensive. Fees for ongoing maintenance and changes to the site are usually based on the amount of work involved. Increasingly, small and medium-size congregations work with companies that provide simple, standard designs (often called templates) for church websites that are inexpensive and easy to set up and maintain. A good website includes photos, audio, video, and whatever information about your church you want to place there—including downloadable documents. The development of a good website takes time, and if you do not have a site now, the process should not be rushed. But the value of a Web presence cannot be underestimated. In the same way people in your city and neighborhood find your church on the Web, clergy looking for a new pastoral call will also find you. No longer does a church reach out solely to people in its neighborhood. Its reach can be worldwide. Former members can follow the ministries of a church they were once a part of. People searching for a church can find your congregation online and read about its teaching, programs, staff, services, and more—all making a first impression before a visitor sets foot inside the door. And pastors anywhere can find your website and learn about your search—and form a first impression.

You may have a gifted computer expert in your congregation who can help develop a website. Designing an effective site requires talent and expertise and dozens of decisions about software platforms, colors, fonts, navigation, flow, look and feel, and content. Members of your congregation may work in organizations that have websites, or may even have their own websites, and a query in the church bulletin should easily yield referrals to qualified designers. Conducting a careful Web search should enable you to find a website designer if you do not have someone in your church qualified to design and maintain the site.

Marketing Your Church on the Web

The key to marketing your church and its search process on the Web is making information available through a multitude of websites and forums. You want to create buzz. This can be accomplished in many ways.

Start by adding information to your church's website about your search efforts. It can be one long page or several pages with unique material on each page. Include an introduction to the search committee, the committee's goals and projected timeline, contact names with phone numbers and e-mail addresses, and links to the church information package and the pastoral questionnaire. Then make sure the website information on your church size, staff, facility, worship, ministries, building, and ministry plans is up to date.

You can also add videos of worship and member activities to the pastoral search pages. Audio can also be used in the form of straight audio files that can be heard online, or podcasts. (A podcast is nothing more than an audio recording that can be downloaded to a computer or device such as an iPod or MP3 player.) Puzzled over what to include? Record several interviews with search committee members about what they are looking for in a pastor, the potential of their church, challenges facing the church, why their church is a good place to be a member and to minister, the history of the church, and more.

Finding Candidates on the Web

Don't forget about advertising on the Web and using it to find pastors seeking a new pastorate. Put an advertisement on your home page and link to another page for more information. The advantage of using a Web-based ad is that you can include links to other pages on your website with audio and video, as well as a contact form. In addition, websites like Ministry Staffing Search can host your ad (for a fee) and provide listings of pastors looking for churches. Websites like Pastoral Search Network, Church Staffing, Church Jobs, and Ministry Staffing Search (see appendix A, "Pastoral Search Resources") offer pastor and church referrals.

Using the Web to Communicate

The Web has made communication between people and organizations easier and faster. E-mails between individuals and groups, online chats, personal and company websites, blogs, and other forms of social media are all designed to help people connect with others.

E-mail Groups

E-mail groups, often called forums, have been around for years. Groups are made up of members with common interests who talk to each other by sending one e-mail that goes to the entire group. They are powerful tools for search committees. Two common e-mail group hosts are:

◆ Yahoo Groups at *Groups.Yahoo.com*
◆ Google Groups at *Groups.Google.com*

With either group, you create an account with a group name, decide whether the group will be public (open to anyone) or private (open only to those whom you invite), and write a description of the group and its purpose. A group created to keep church members informed should be kept private, so that only your church members receive e-mails. Each group has an owner, called the moderator, who oversees the membership. Sending an e-mail to the group name sends it to all members. Depending on how the group is set up, either the moderator or the members can post and respond to e-mails by sending one e-mail to the group name. The conversation among members and church leaders and staff can be helpful to monitor the health of the congregation. While the church secretary might have an e-mail list on his or her computer, creating a group allows members to send e-mails from their own computers, rather than through the church office. Members will know that the group's purpose is only to receive updates on the search process. The search committee could also create a private account that would enable committee members to exchange e-mail among themselves without allowing others to see the messages.

The church secretary or another staff member could work with the search committee to send an e-mail invitation to all church members. The members could then accept the invitation ("opt in") to become part of the group. This useful method of informing members of the search committee's progress should not serve as a substitute for face-to-face updates in Sunday services and on other occasions. If you do not have the e-mail addresses of members, start collecting them. Add new people to the group as you learn their e-mail addresses. The group members can also be sent an e-mail message encouraging them to ask friends and relatives to pass on information about the position and the names of possible pastors to contact. Consider reminding the congregation of the value of e-mail to stay informed, while emphasizing that bulletin and pulpit announcements will continue to be used.

Social Media

Social media have become a huge part of our communications; they offer search teams a unique way to spread the word of their church's pastoral search. In short, social media are online websites where people connect electronically to be part of a virtual social community, gathering around a virtual water cooler. These sites are available twenty-four hours a day to people around the world and are free to anyone who already has an Internet account. Social media include blogs, Twitter, Facebook, Plaxo, LinkedIn, Digg, Delicious, Fark, Mixx, Newsvine, Reddit, StumbleUpon, Tumblr—even YouTube.

Social networking sites let you add links to draw people back to your website. Common to most social media sites is the "user profile"—personal information you post so that readers know a bit about you. When the site is used for a church account, a photo of the church or a group of its members and other church information are given instead of personal data.

The power of social media is in creating an ever-growing circle of people who "know" other people, one or more of whom can help you find a pastor. It's all about exposure. Someone you do not know becomes a part of your network, and that person may know of a pastor in a neighboring church who is interested in a new church leadership position. It's cheap marketing. Social media offers one more source for pastors to find information about your congregation and its search.

Talk with your committee members to determine whether any of them use social media in their work or personal lives. If so, ask one or two of these members to investigate which of the social media outlets mentioned below would be beneficial for your search efforts. Ask too if they would be willing to assist the search committee with setting up accounts and training staff and committee members in using the chosen medium.

Only a few social-media websites are relevant for our search efforts. Whichever form you use, do a Web search for "how to use *[name]*" to find online resources and tips about using that medium. Here is a look at four forms that can be effectively used in your search efforts.

Blogs

Blogs (an abbreviation of "web logs") are websites composed of a series of entries, often on a particular subject, typically posted every few days. The blog owner establishes the blog, chooses the title and theme, and posts (writes) content. Usually blog posts are relatively short, no more than five hundred words. New posts are always shown first, but readers can click on links to older posts. The blog owner chooses whether to allow readers to post comments. Links can be added from your blog to other websites (including your church's), and vice versa. Blogs can include images, audio, and video.

Blogs are easy to establish and take little skill or knowledge to maintain. There are several free blog hosts, the most popular being *WordPress.com* and *Blogger.com*. *Typepad.com* is a blog host that charges a small yearly fee but offers the ability to easily customize your blog.

An alternative is to add a blog to your church's website. Your website host may offer a blog feature; if not, WordPress offers (at *WordPress.org*) fully customizable, free blog software that you can add to your host site, the same software used at *WordPress.com*. Your church's webmaster can install the WordPress blogging software on your website and customize it to meet your needs.

A blog can be a powerful tool; it can be used to provide updates on your search process. With a subscription service through *FeedBurner.com* or *FeedBlitz.com*, church members can sign up for updates as you post new material. Blog posts can be sent as e-mail every few days, once a week, or as news and events happen. Post news about your interim pastor, the creation of the church information packet, how many pastors you are talking with, news from your meetings, and more. It's easy to overlook e-mail in busy inboxes. Having a blog dedicated to your search efforts makes it easy for people to bookmark the site and return time after time. Blog posts remain on the blog page and can be read at any time. An advantage of having a blog rather than simply using e-mail is that search engines "love" blogs—creating a search blog will increase the chances that pastors and others find the site and learn about your search. Two important parts of blogs are the links in the posts to other Web pages and sites, and the opportunity for readers to respond to a post. These comments can help the committee, church staff, and board members keep their fingers on the pulse of the congregation. Keep in mind, however, that anything posted on a blog can be viewed by *anyone*. Much of what the search committee does is confidential, so be sure to post only news that is intended to be public.

When you use a blog to spread word of your search, one person is designated as the "owner" and the person who adds the new posts. It could be the search committee secretary or the church secretary. Members of the search committee, and even board members, can write material to be posted by this person.

Facebook

Facebook *(Facebook.com)* is a networking site, and the number of individuals who use Facebook is growing daily. Users create their own personalized page and then send invitations to those they know, or want to know, to be "friends." Facebook's value is an ever-widening circle of online "friends," as people recommend others they think you should know. Once anyone accepts your invitation, that person receives information as you post it. Others may "friend" you too. Once you have a personal Facebook account, you can create a church account called a "group" and invite members to join the group. Each person must establish a Facebook account to access the group.

Your church members are your first intended audience. The second audience is anyone who you think would be helpful in your search efforts. This can include pastors you know who might have contacts and who could give you names of other pastors to consider in your search. Posting information is easy. Access your church's Facebook page and type whatever you want into the box. It is then viewable by anyone who is your Facebook "friend." As friends read your post, they can write comments, which all your friends can see.

Not everyone checks Facebook daily, and e-mail can be quicker, but Facebook has value for a search committee. The ability to use Facebook to connect with others who know others can lead you to people who can help you find pastors seeking a new church family. Post only the information you want others to see.

LinkedIn

LinkedIn *(LinkedIn.com)* offers professionals a place to meet, network, link up through the recommendations of others, and search for jobs and employees. Each committee member should create a personal account and add information to his or her profile page. When you create your profile, make sure you add your church's website, your search committee membership, and related information, so that the profile reflects your search involvement.

Once you have set up an account, you can start a group for your church and spread the word about your search. Click on "Groups" and then on "Create a Group." Add your group information and invite members of the team. You can also join existing groups by clicking on "Groups" on the left side of the screen and searching by topic. When you find a related group, join it to connect with the members. As always, the more members the group has, the wider the contact possibilities.

LinkedIn offers applications for holding group discussions, conducting polls, sending personalized invitations, and making introductions. Another great application is Huddle Workspace. It allows you to create a private group for hosting discussions and virtual meetings, sharing candidate information, and sharing confidential files. You can post short updates or pose questions to the group. LinkedIn provides a secure, private online workspace to communicate as a group. Simply use Huddle Workspace for virtual online meetings. Committee members need their own accounts.

One important benefit of LinkedIn is that it allows you to see who knows whom and who can make an introduction. These connections can provide leads to potential pastors and others in contact with clergy who might be interested in a church move.

YouTube

YouTube *(YouTube.com)* is the primary website for sharing videos. Although not designed as a search engine, it has become the second-largest information search engine, after Google. Users create accounts and upload videos. They can then link to the videos from other websites or blogs, or include the link in e-mails and in other social media activities. YouTube videos provide an easy way to give viewers a taste of your church in action. Videos can include worship and other church

CHART 3.1. Task Cluster: Using the Internet

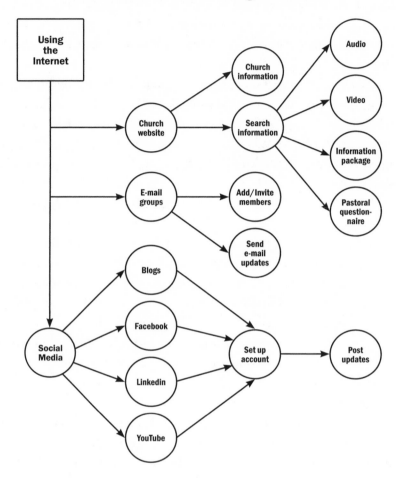

activities, a tour of your facilities, families telling stories, your board or search team talking about your church—anything that might paint a picture of your church for whoever finds the video. Each video page includes a "comments" section where any viewer can add a short note. A page-views feature shows how many times the video has been watched.

Well made, high-quality videos can be useful tools to present your church and its ministries. When you add videos to YouTube, put them on your church's website too. However, if you do not have a church website and you know someone with experience uploading videos, YouTube is a good alternative.

The Web has the power both to expand the range of your search and to keep church members informed. A well-designed church website showcases your church, its ministries, and its people, which is important when attempting to attract pastors looking for a new pastoral opportunity. A well-planned systematic use of e-mail and a blog can ensure that your congregation and friends of your church are informed and connected to your search efforts. LinkedIn can help search committee members stay connected. Social media can open doors to others beyond your church walls, maybe one of whom knows a pastor who is a good match for your church. Give the Web a chance to enhance your search efforts.

Chapter 4

◆ ◆ ◆

Managing
the Congregation

The congregation needs to know the basics of what the pastoral search committee is doing. Not all the details need to be shared, but members do need to know where you are in the process of finding a pastor. A congregation that is uninformed is often confused or unsupportive. Tell members that you have reviewed "x" number of profiles, have scheduled interviews, and have moved "x" number of pastors into the next stage of the process. In addition, the search committee chair, or other key person, needs to keep the congregation informed with periodic status reports. This updating can be done with inserts in the Sunday bulletin, announcements in the Sunday morning worship service, postings on your church's website and blog, e-mail messages, and your choices of social media. Remember not to compromise confidentiality standards. The sample bulletin insert below shows how information can be shared.

◆ ◆ ◆

PASTORAL SEARCH COMMITTEE REPORT
UPDATES FOR DECEMBER 13
Our search process includes various stages through which the pastors under consideration move. Stage I involves gathering information on pastors and sending them our church information packet. In Stage II we review pastoral profiles and candidates' responses to

our questionnaire. In Stage III we listen to sermon tapes and conduct reference checks. Finally, in Stage IV we interview pastors. We are working with people at all four of these stages.

Stage IV. Interviews

Interviews have been arranged with two pastors who have advanced to this stage.

Stage III. Sermon Tapes and Reference Checks

We are talking to the people whose names were provided to us as references by five pastors. Sermon tapes have been requested; three have been received so far and are being reviewed.

Stage II. Pastoral Profiles and Questionnaires

We have reviewed the pastoral questionnaires of two other pastors, and one has moved to stage III.

Stage I. Sharing and Gathering Information

We are at stage I with two pastors who have been sent packets of information about our church and who are completing our questionnaire and sending sermon tapes.

We have discussed twenty-two other pastors and have found that they are not open to a move at this time or are not a good match for us.

Next Steps

Our next meeting on January 9 will focus on the pastors' visiting schedule and the selection process.

◆ ◆ ◆

Keeping the congregation informed can be simple, but not everyone wants the same quantity of information. Some just want to know that the committee is doing its job. Others want to know that the committee has talked to the pastor they recommended. A few will want to know everything. All search committee members need to be mindful of confidentiality issues when sharing information about the search. Remember that the names of pastors under consideration should not be shared with the congregation. Use a weekly bulletin announcement like the one below and add it to your congregation's website and social media outlets to keep communications lines open.

◆ ◆ ◆

PASTORAL SEARCH QUESTIONS

Any member of the search committee would be happy to provide answers to your questions about the search, potential pastors, time frames, and the call process. Just ask one of us. *[Include your names and telephone numbers.]* When formal reports are made to the congregation, our chair will take the lead. Otherwise, any committee member can answer general questions.

◆ ◆ ◆

When the search process has reached the point of selecting a potential pastor, more information needs to be given to the congregation. Members need to know the dates pastors will be visiting and should be encouraged to be present to hear them and meet them. People also need to know how the pastor will be selected and the dates of any planned congregational meetings. Create a handout for the congregation, and post information to your website and social media outlets describing the selection process, who has been selected, the visiting schedule, and the date of the congregational meeting. Include a page about each pastor that contains information on the pastor's gifts, strengths, and ministry style; his or her thoughts on worship, leadership, education, evangelism, and fellowship; his or her pastoral history; a family profile; and a family picture (if available). More information on this step in the search can be found in chapter 11, "Presenting Your Best Side."

Creative Communications

The search committee will use many methods to keep the congregation informed. Bulletin announcements and updates from the pulpit have been mentioned previously. But there are other creative ways.

A search committee brochure or leaflet introducing each committee member with a photo, a brief biographical sketch, and contact information can be distributed to church members. The brochure should also briefly explain the search process and search committee covenant.

If a bulletin board is located in a central location in the church building, create an attractive, readable display that includes the search committee mandate, the search committee member list, relevant data from your congregational survey, and updates on the search.

A chart that shows the steps in a search will help members understand what is happening and enable them to visualize where the search committee is in the overall process. Hang the chart in a high-traffic space, so that everyone has an opportunity to see it each week. Use pushpins or markers to show progress and milestones.

Each of the examples above should be duplicated on your church's website and social-media outlets. The Web presence of your church can be far-reaching and should be used whenever possible.

Chapter 3, "Using the Internet," has more information on using a website, e-mail, and social media to keep the congregation informed.

Filling the Pulpit

Make sure your Sunday worship is fulfilling and meaningful during the pastoral vacancy. This is a good time to invite other clergy to preach. Your board is responsible for filling the pulpit on Sundays. If you do not have elders or deacons or other lay leaders who can lead worship, or if your polity does not allow that, other ordained ministers must be used. Guest pastors typically only lead Sunday worship, while an interim pastor can fill the pulpit and assist with most other aspects of church life. If you do not employ an interim pastor, you will need to use weekly guest pastors, at your congregation's expense. Guest pastors may be staff at a church with multiple pastors, retired pastors, or clergy not serving a parish and assigned by a regional office to provide service for one Sunday. An elder or worship leader will need to work with guest pastors to coordinate the elements of the worship services as necessary. Four Sundays a month could cost from $600 to $1,000, depending on the number of services and the location of the congregation. This amount includes the pulpit-supply fee and mileage expense. Assume that you will pay a full-time interim pastor approximately the same salary and benefits as your previous full-time pastor. If you use a part-time interim pastor, your expenses would be less. (Chapter 2, "The Interim Period," has more information on interim support.)

The Grieving Process

Another important aspect of managing a congregation during the call process is dealing with the congregation's grief over the departure of the previous pastor. When a pastor leaves a church, members and friends will have an array of emotions to deal with. Some may be in denial that their pastor would consider leaving. Others may feel anger when they realize that the pastor is leaving, guilt if they feel some burden of personal responsibility for his or her departure, fear of what may happen to their church—or relief, if they did not like that pastor. Some people may even become depressed. Others may pull away from the church and ultimately leave. This grieving process is normal.

The search committee needs to work with the board to ensure that the congregation's grieving process is managed well. Assistance may be needed from your church counselor or supervisor, neighboring pastors, or, if necessary, a trained counselor. Members need to come to terms with their emotional ties to the former pastor. If there are critical unresolved issues from the previous pastor's tenure that involve members or friends of the congregation, they need to be resolved.

The leaders of the church in particular need to be sensitive to the need of members to grieve. They should encourage open communication between the board and the congregation, and among members. Visits or telephone calls should be made to members who need special attention. Help members talk through their feelings and work through unresolved issues. Arrange for counseling when necessary. Realize that this grieving process is needed to allow individuals to attain closure with their feelings for their previous pastor. Allowing people to grieve will help them make a fresh start and develop a good relationship with the new pastor.

While members' grief is more the concern of the board than of the search committee, unresolved grief can hinder the work of the search committee if it is not managed well. It can adversely influence the results of congregational surveys and affect your list of qualities desired in a new pastor. Search committee members, in particular, need to be aware of their own grief and deal with it early in the search.

When the congregation's grief is being managed effectively, the search committee can begin its self-study of the board, the congregation, and the ministries of the church. This process is important to ensure a good match with your next pastor.

CHART 4.1. Task Cluster: Managing the Congregation

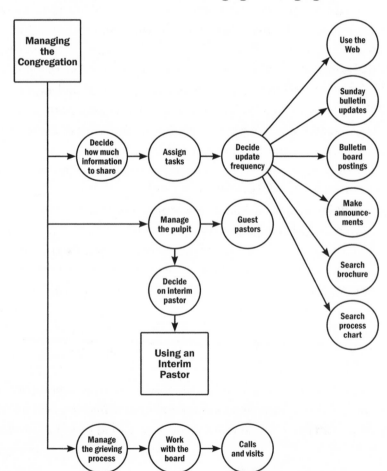

Chapter 5

◆ ◆ ◆

Determining Who You Are

The information you present about your church, including its leadership, membership, and ministries must be as thorough and accurate as possible. Surveyed pastors offered the following perspectives about what churches had said about themselves. Consider their comments as you think about determining who you are.

- "I preferred churches with a vision, purpose, and goals— churches that knew who they were and where they hoped to go."
- "They knew who they were and presented that information in a customized church profile and church packet."
- "They did not always identify all of the informal leadership. This led to problems later."
- "They did not identify their weaknesses. They did not mislead in their impressions—they simply did not have the answers to give."

The Importance of Determining Who You Are

One of the most important tasks your pastoral search committee will undertake is a self-study of the board, congregation, and ministries of the church. It is certainly not the task of only the search committee to work through all of these issues, and therefore the board needs to be directly involved in this process. The study is necessary to portray your church accurately to prospective pastors through your information packet and in other communications. Use this study to identify the church's strengths and weaknesses as well as other characteristics. Knowing these can help in determining the strengths and skills you need in your next pastor. This should be done through an information-gathering process managed by the search committee. The information provided to pastors will give them a definitive statement of your focus, needs, and priorities. Do not paint a false picture of who you are. Anything incorrect may surface when the pastor comes to be interviewed or, worse, after she accepts and finds that things are not as rosy as the picture initially portrayed. Then she and the board will have to work through the issues.

Remember that pastors will read your church packet in the same way you read their pastoral profiles. As you read between the lines, so will they. As you are alert for red flags, so are they. As you check references, so may they. Let your creative juices flow as you build your church packet and make a church video, but be both complete and realistic. Consider the following questions in determining who you are as a church:

+ What is unique about our congregation?
+ What is unique about our opportunities for ministry?
+ What are the strengths and weaknesses of our congregation?
+ To what degree are we open to change? How do we convey our openness or lack of openness?
+ What challenges can we offer to a pastor?
+ What in our past would help as we look ahead at new challenges?
+ What are the vision and mission of our church, and does our congregation claim them?
+ What core values shape our ministries?
+ What is our view on outreach, and do our actions support this view?
+ What ministries need to be started or developed more fully?
+ What needs do we anticipate over the next five years?

- Is our church willing to learn from and follow the leadership of a new pastor?
- What professional qualities and attributes are we looking for in a pastor?

Talk to your board about any existing vision, mission, and core-values statements the congregation has. Are they current? Can the majority of the congregation recognize the stated visions and values as being the ones this congregation has? Do the documents need to be reworked? While the search committee focuses on the self-study, the board should focus on these statements.

Many churches today are more diverse than in earlier years. Churches often include people of many nationalities and cultures, wide differences in ages, members who have switched from one denomination to another, and people with no previous church background. Any one of these can present challenges to a pastor. Finding the right match between a pastor and a diverse congregation can be complex. It is important to identify the leadership qualities and any special skills required. These expectations then need to be presented effectively to interested pastors. Examples include training in ministry to specific age groups, experience in missions and outreach, and experience in leading large or multicultural churches.

An area that is becoming more important in the search process is the identification of styles and issues that, if unacknowledged in the search process, could affect the relationship between the church and a new pastor. Two main issues are worship style and leadership approach. A question in many churches is whether women may serve as deacons or elders, or in a pastoral position. Failure to identify and communicate these issues could lead to problems in the relationship between the pastor and the board, or the pastor and the congregation. A pastor who is used to leading by himself could end up with problems in a church where the board had become accustomed to sharing leadership with its former pastor. Similarly, a pastor who promotes "seeker-sensitive" worship services will feel stifled in a congregation that prefers formal liturgical worship. Be aware of distinctive styles and issues in your church and describe them in your church profile and in the church information packet distributed to prospective pastors. You will also want to ask questions about such issues in your pastoral questionnaire.

Your congregation might use the self-study process to clarify other aspects of your ministry. For example, some churches have several pastors. There may be a senior pastor, a youth pastor, a pastor of evangelism, and a pastor of congregational care. Other churches may call a pastor for a mission-field ministry. Another church may call a pastor to be a college or military chaplain or to be a pastor in an industrial ministry. If you are calling a pastor to a specialized ministry, think through the needs you hope the new pastor will help you address and your specific expectations about that pastor's role. By identifying your special pastoral needs, you will make it easier for pastors to decide whether your ministry needs could fit their experience, gifts, and skills.

By conducting a self-study and identifying the congregation's styles and issues, you will take the first step toward ensuring a potentially good match with a new pastor. The second step is to clarify your expectations of your new pastor. Will she be expected to do counseling, serve on five committees, and teach Sunday school and midweek Bible studies? Does he expect board members to lead the committees? Members may have a wide range of expectations regarding commitment, involvement, and accountability. The document sample "Pastoral Roles, Responsibilities, and Relationships" in appendix B is one tool you can use to clarify pastoral expectations. Similar tools can be created for board members and the congregation. Care taken in these two steps can help prevent problems with relationships later in the life of the pastor, the board, and congregation.

Creating Your Congregational Survey

A congregational survey, the most commonly used self-study method, will provide information about your church that you need to know. It will help as you compare the ministries, needs, and challenges of your church against the skills and experience of pastors interested in your church. In appendix C you'll find a sample congregational survey, which can be modified to fit your congregation's requirements. The survey covers five specific areas:

- Information about the person completing the survey.
- Professional qualities we desire in our next pastor.
- Our expectations of our next pastor.
- Strengths, weaknesses, and needs of our congregation.
- Congregational interests—what is important to us.

There are many reasons to do a congregational survey. You will want to conduct one if:

- You do not know the demographics of your congregation.
- Your are uncertain of the professional qualities you desire in your next pastor.
- You are unsure of the congregation's expectations of a new pastor's involvements in the congregation and the community.
- You cannot identify the needs in your congregation.
- You cannot identify your congregation's strengths and weaknesses.

If your church has recently completed a similar survey or has gone through a master-planning or strategic-planning effort, this survey may not be necessary. If you conduct a congregational survey anyway, compare the results with your master-planning or strategic-planning summaries to determine whether all areas are covered and whether the results match. If the results do not match, take the time to find the correct information by talking to key people, taking another survey, or inviting the congregation to an open forum. Once a survey is completed and tabulated, post the results for the congregation to see.

An alternative to a paper survey is a Web-based survey tool such as SurveyMonkey *(surveymonkey.com)*. Other Web-based survey sites include Zoomerang *(zoomerang.com)*, InstantSurvey *(instantsurvey.com)*, and QuestionPro *(questionpro.com)*. Although SurveyMonkey offers a free version, it is too limited for a congregational self-study.

For about $20 a month, you can conduct an online survey with unlimited questions and up to one thousand monthly responses. A Web-based survey allows for a custom thank-you page, provides live results, and includes a printable PDF file of the results. This saves your compiling the results, which you must do with a paper survey. You could use the service for three or four months to conduct your survey and then close the account. Otherwise, a survey account costs about $200 a year. With online survey tools, you create your questions and determine the length of the survey and how long it runs. Once the survey is designed, simply e-mail the Web link to your members or let them know the link in a letter or bulletin.

The Church-Profile Form

If your congregation is affiliated with a denomination, you may find that the denomination has a church-profile form. Request a copy and review it to be sure your survey asks for all the information needed to complete the church-profile form. When you have completed your self-study, you should be able to complete the profile, describing your church and the qualities of the pastor you are seeking. Use this church-profile form to prepare your church information packet. You will also submit copies of the completed form to the required denominational or regional offices. Staff will use this form to determine which pastors' names to give your congregation for consideration. Finally, your board should be given a copy for its records.

If your congregation is not part of a denomination that has a church-profile form, use the questions below as a guide to compile the information typically included in a profile. Again, the information will be helpful as you develop your church information packet. The typical church-profile form asks for basic information about your church:

- What is the size of the staff? What are the staff members' titles, and do they work full time or part time?
- What is the size and composition of the board, including gender breakdown, and who serves on the board (elders, deacons, or committee leaders)?
- What are your vision, mission, and core values?

- What are your current and future congregational goals?
- What are the church membership numbers for the past ten years, including the median age of members and a rough age breakdown with percentages?
- What is your style of worship, how many services do you have, and how many attend each service?
- What is your church's education program, and what curriculum do you use?
- What programs are offered for children, youth, college-age singles, and adults?
- What is your current outreach and missions program, and whom does it involve?

Other questions may ask about your facilities and budget:
- What is the present budget and the amount of indebtedness?
- Do you usually meet your yearly budget, and by what percentage are you under or over?
- What is the condition of the church facilities?
- Does the church own a parsonage?
- Is it an option for the pastor to own his or her own home?

Be able to identify the specifics about the congregation and the community:
- What are the congregation's strengths and weaknesses?
- What are the congregation's ministries?
- What are the needs of the community?
- What is your involvement in the community?
- What are your outreach ministries?
- What ecumenical ministries is the church involved in?
- What is the racial, ethnic, and economic makeup of the community?

Finally, congregations are asked to answer questions about their next pastor:
- What are the personal and professional qualities you desire in your next pastor?

◆ What priorities would you like your next pastor to focus on?

◆ What is your compensation package, in general terms? (Depending on your denomination's policies, this may or may not be asked.)

As the search committee goes through the self-study process and conducts a congregational survey, its members are forming an excellent base of knowledge about their church and its ministries. The next step in the search process is to use this information to create a church information packet.

CHART 5.1. Task Cluster: Determining Who You Are

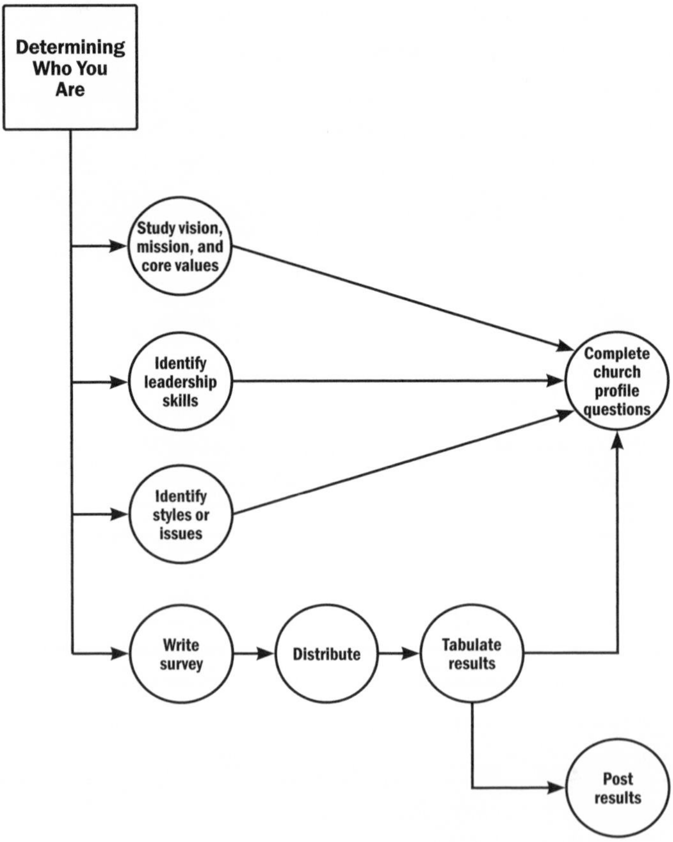

Chapter 6

◆ ◆ ◆

The Church
Information Packet

A church information packet contains everything an interested pastor needs to know about your congregation. It must help potential candidates get to know your church and want to explore further the possibility of becoming your next pastor.

You need to create an attractive, distinctive church information package. It must present an accurate picture of your congregation that grabs the interest of a pastor and makes him or her want to learn more about it. Creating such a packet may take several weeks and many hours of work by various people in your church, but it will speak volumes about the congregation's identity. Above all else, be honest in your representation of your church, its ministries, and its strengths and needs. Think about how you can express what is unique to your church—something that sets it apart from other churches. Build on this unique element.

Creating an Excellent Package

There is a saying in advertising: "Presentation is everything." While your packet can be created on your own computer using a type font like Helvetica on Word for Windows software, it will not look as professional as it should. Rather than save a few dollars, make the effort to create a well-made, informative, professional-quality document that showcases your church. As you create your document, investigate whether your church has members who are experienced in desktop publishing. Software programs like Microsoft's Publisher, Adobe's In-Design, or Apple's Pages can be used to create a professional-looking document that includes text, photos, images, and charts. All the material can be incorporated in a colorful document that will set your church apart from others. An alternative is to use an outside vendor to create the document. Once it has been created, convert it into a PDF document and add it to your website. Print several color copies and put each one in a binder. Put the binders in the church lobby for church members to review. If your church has a webmaster, check with that person, since often he or she can help create the package.

Quality can also be demonstrated in other ways. Send your packets by Priority Mail. This will cost about one-third as much as Express Mail and yet be delivered in two to three days. Include a similar self-addressed, stamped envelope for the return of the package if the pastor has no interest in your query. If there are forms or questionnaires for the pastor to return if interested, be sure to add a self-addressed, stamped envelope. Let candidates know that the forms are available on your website to save filling them out by hand. Be clear, direct, and concise as you write the material in your packet. Make sure it is well organized. By presenting a professional-quality packet, you will demonstrate that you care about your congregation and its ministries.

What to Include

You might begin developing your information packet by asking how much material you need to include. Another way to approach the task is to think about what you want to say about your church. What would be important for a stranger to know about the congregation? Make a list of what should be included. Realize that other churches are also creating church information packets to send to pastors. Remember that putting too little in a church information packet is worse than putting too much.

First, create a brochure that includes a description and photo of your church, contact information, your mission and/or vision statements, and a brief personal sketch and photo of each search committee member. Then add information that describes your board, congregation, ministries, and community. The areas described below are basic to providing a complete picture of who you are as a church. Ideally, put information about each area on a page, writing enough about each to satisfy the pastor—who, you have to assume, knows nothing about your church. Consider using a folder with a three-hole paper clasp in the center and pockets on either side. Standard three-hole-punched sheets can be placed in the center section, and smaller brochures or booklets will fit in the pockets. This type of folder best displays the material you will send. Make a table of contents and use tabbed dividers to separate sections.

Much of this information can be gathered through congregational surveys, strategic-planning documents, church brochures, board minutes, the church website, and area profiles from newspapers and local business associations. Church bulletins, newsletters, special-events programs, and membership directories will complete your information files.

Our Vision, Mission, and Goals

If your church has vision or mission statements, include them in the packet. Some churches have a statement of core values. Other statements that guide ministries or committees can also be included. These all serve to show what guides the congregation. If you have goals for the church and its committees, review and update any that are outdated or have been found to be unrealistic, and include the revised material in the packet.

Our Worship Style

Identify your worship style. Is it traditional, contemporary, or a mix? Do you use traditional hymns or newer praise songs? Is the singing accompanied by a pipe organ, piano, electronic keyboard, or CD player with prerecorded music? Or is the singing unaccompanied? Are there choirs or praise teams? Is there a song leader? Do you use a band in worship? Do you include multimedia? Are hymn and song texts projected on a screen, or printed in a hymnal or worship bulletin? Who plans worship? Does someone other than the pastor lead portions of the service?

Congregational Life

Describe the makeup of your congregation and congregational life. Include the number of worship services and how many people typically attend each service (distinguishing between members and visitors, if possible); days and times of all worship services, Sunday school, and youth and singles groups; membership statistics; percentages of members and visitors who have been affiliated with your church for various lengths of time; age makeup of the congregation; percentages of members living various distances from the church; the cultural and ethnic groups represented; and the mix of occupations or professions of members. If your denomination has a standard profile form, use it. Otherwise, present this information in a format that matches the rest of the packet.

Our Strengths and Weaknesses

Identify known strengths and weaknesses of the congregation, using data from your congregational survey and self-analysis. You should be able to list at least six strengths and four weaknesses. Be honest. Focus on the strengths more than on the weaknesses. Any distinctive challenges facing the congregation can also be noted here. If there are divisive problems in the church, identify them, so that they do not come as a surprise to an incoming pastor.

Pastoral Roles, Responsibilities, Relationships, and Needs

If you have a pastoral job description or other guidelines, include them here. Appendix B, "Sample Pastoral Roles, Responsibilities, and Relationships," identifies areas of leadership, authority, commitment, vision development, personal giftedness, the work of equipping and enabling, and relationships to board, staff, and committee leaders. This important section helps a pastor understand his or her areas of responsibility, especially in comparison to the leadership responsibilities of the board, other staff, and committee leaders. Are you looking for a pastor to be your leader, equipper, or counselor? To teach certain Christian education classes? Identify areas of specialized pastoral ministry for which he or she will be responsible. Identify your pastoral ministry needs in worship, leadership, congregational care, fellowship, and outreach. Identify other areas that may be relevant to your congregation. If you have completed a standard denominational profile form, this section may duplicate some information there, but it can be helpful to pastors to hear about your pastoral needs in your own words.

Our Structure

Provide an overview of your church's organization. Identify the structure and size of the board and its composition. Outline how staff members relate to the board and other groups in the congregation. Explain your committee structure. If you have an organizational chart, include it here. It may be a formal, computer-generated flowchart or a simple, hand-drawn picture. Either way, it is helpful for a pastor to see the reporting and organizational structure of the board and the committees responsible for various ministries. If you have any policy manuals or other organizational guidelines, briefly discuss them.

Board Roles, Responsibilities, and Relationships

If you have any guidelines or standards for board members, identify them. It can be helpful for a pastor to know the standards to which board members are held accountable. Does the pastor or a board member chair the board? Does the board exercise oversight of the pastor? If you have a pastoral relations committee, explain what function that group serves. If the role of women in the church is an issue, identify your congregation's position on women serving in leadership roles on the board and elsewhere in the congregation.

Staff Roles, Responsibilities, and Relationships

In this section, introduce your staff (provide a brief biography and photo of each person), the hours they work, and to whom they are accountable. Staff members should have well defined job descriptions. Include what they are responsible for, to whom they report, and by whom they are supervised. It is helpful for a pastor to know ahead of time what staff oversight roles he or she may have.

Committee Leader Roles, Responsibilities, and Relationships

Detail the standards under which committee leaders operate. To whom are they responsible and accountable? How are their roles defined?

Member Roles, Responsibilities, and Relationships

To what standards are members held? Are there areas of ministry, commitment, accountability, and relationships? How does one become a member? What are the benefits and responsibilities of being a member?

Friends of the Congregation

If you have any statements or guidelines for nonmember friends of the congregation, identify them. Provide some information about the number of individuals and families who attend regularly but have not formally joined the church.

Our Ministries

List all the ministries of your church with a brief description of each. Consider church school or Sunday school, vacation Bible school, the church's preschool, boys' and girls' clubs, junior-high and high-school youth groups, children's worship, Bible studies, fellowship groups, women's and men's groups, outreach programs, and youth and adult choirs.

Our Facilities

Describe your facilities. What is the seating capacity of the sanctuary? How many classrooms are there? What is the size of the fellowship hall? How up-to-date are the facilities? Is there off-street parking? Does the church own any other property? Are there any building or expansion plans in the works? Have the facilities been adequately maintained? Is any major maintenance work needed? Include both interior and exterior photos of the church facilities.

Our Finances

What is the annual budget? Is it usually met? By what percentage has giving exceeded or fallen short of expenses for last year and the current year? If possible, include a current giving and income summary. Describe trends in giving patterns over the past five years. Identify the major pieces of the budget picture. Are there any outstanding debts, and if so, what are the anticipated time frames to pay them off? Include any current financial efforts such as increasing giving or tithing awareness.

Our Pastoral Compensation Policy

Some churches follow compensation standards set by their denomination. Others build their own compensation packages. What source has been used to establish guidelines for pastoral salary and benefits? What is included in benefits? What expenses are reimbursed? Are time and money for continuing education built into the package? How much vacation is offered, and is there opportunity for a sabbatical? Is there a parsonage? If so, include photos and details. Is the board willing to discuss the pastor's receiving a housing allowance and owning his or her own home? If a finance committee manages the compensation package, be sure your information is current. Determine whether you want to provide fixed numbers or a range at this time, or wait until a call is issued to provide specific figures for each part of the proposed compensation package.

Our History

Write a page or two about the history of your church. In narrative format, tell what has happened. Identify previous pastors and years of service. What events have shaped the congregation, the mission, and the vision? Have there been building projects? If you have a church historian, ask him or her to write a history of the congregation. Some churches have church anniversary booklets that include a history.

Our Community

Describe your community. In what kind of neighborhood is the church located? What similar churches are nearby? Tell a bit about the area— is it urban, suburban, rural, industrial, inner city? What Christian and public schools are available? Are there any colleges or universities nearby? What opportunities exist for the arts, sports, and outdoor activities? What is the range of weather through the year? Consider including a map of the local area. Go online to find a map that can be pasted into a document. If you can afford it, consider getting demographic data for your area to complete the community profile.

Search Committee, Board, and Staff Information

List the members of the search committee, the board, and the staff by name and title. A photo and a few sentences about each person's role in the congregation will help identify them. Include the phone numbers or e-mail addresses only for those individuals designated as contacts.

Additional Materials

The material below can be added to the pockets on the sides of the folder. Select materials appropriate for your church:
- A church brochure.
- Two or three recent bulletins or programs.
- Two or three recent church newsletters.

◆ A church membership directory, preferably one with pictures.
◆ Brochures about the church's ministries.
◆ Bulletins from the church's special Christmas, Easter, or other musical programs.
◆ A DVD as described below.
◆ Brochures from local Christian schools.
◆ A pastoral questionnaire (if allowed by your denomination) that the pastor can complete if she is interested in continuing communications, and a return envelope. Attach a note that the questionnaire is available online.
◆ An addressed and stamped envelope for the return of the packet if the pastor believes that your church is not a good fit for his gifts and pastoral skills. If your packet does not contain photos, programs, directories, DVDs, CDs, or other hard-to-replace items, you might skip asking for return of the packet.

If possible, have a member of your congregation make a video to include in your information packet. A well-made video will show more about your church and congregational life to candidates than any other medium. Include highlights from church activities: choir practices, youth and children's programs, fellowship groups, vacation Bible school, church school or Sunday school, choir cantatas, casual interviews with church members, and views of the church grounds, facilities, and the parsonage. Introduce board members and search committee members. Consider videotaping the board talking about the church and its ministries, and the search committee members talking about what the search means to them. Be sure the search committee sees the video, so that its members know what the candidates are seeing. Keep the running time under an hour. Use DVD format, since most computers can play these disks, and many people have DVD players.

Make at least ten of these packages. Have them ready to go, pre-stamped, so that all you have to add is the address. You can easily have ten or more packages out for review at one time. If more packages are necessary, make additional copies. Remember to keep originals of all the materials. Consider making several copies of your final packet available to the congregation for members' review.

Introducing the Packet

Write a cover letter to introduce the packet and specify when a member of the search committee will follow up. Use church letterhead. A sample letter:

◆ ◆ ◆

Greetings from Anytown Community Church!

Thank you for being willing to review material our search committee has compiled about Anytown Community Church. We hope this packet will provide a clear picture of our church.

Following this letter is an Anytown Community Church profile. We trust it will provide answers to your questions.

In the side pockets of this folder are copies of Anytown Community Church brochures, recent Sunday bulletins, two recent monthly newsletters, and information on local Christian schools. A forty-minute video provides a glimpse of our congregation in action.

If you feel positive about our ministries and would like to pursue discussions, please complete the pastoral questionnaire and send it to us in the envelope provided. If possible, send a photo of yourself, or of you and your family.

If, however, after reviewing this package, you do not wish to pursue discussions with us, please use the enclosed self-addressed, stamped envelope to return the materials to us. We appreciate your time considering Anytown Community Church.

A member of the pastoral search committee will be contacting you within ten days. We pray that through this search process, both you and we will find a match that will honor God and further his kingdom here on earth.

◆ ◆ ◆

Modify the letter as appropriate based on constraints or special procedures of your denomination.

With your church information packet completed, you have a powerful resource to send to pastors, who will be able to learn much from it about your members, ministries, and facilities. The next step is to identify pastors who might be candidates. Rarely do they come to you. You need to find them.

CHART 6.1. Task Cluster: The Church Information Packet

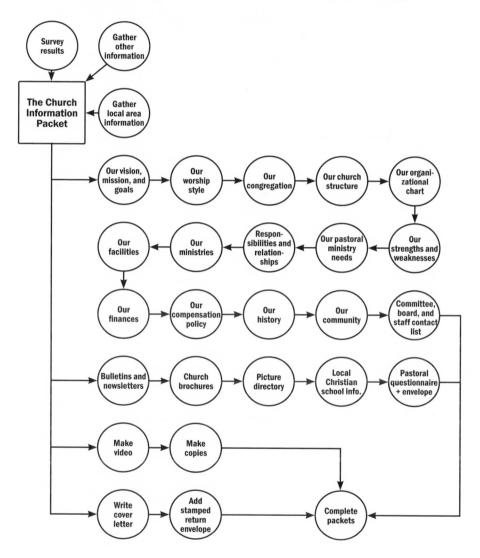

Chapter 7

◆ ◆ ◆

Finding Candidates

If your denominational practices permit congregations to solicit the names of prospective pastors independently, there are many sources for candidates that your search committee might consider. You can place search announcements in the church bulletin, in regional and denominational publications, and in religious magazines or newsletters with a wider audience. You can also speak with the pastors you know and ask them for the names of potential candidates.

Run an announcement in your bulletin and on your website asking members to submit the names of pastors they know personally or whose preaching they have heard, or pastors they have heard about from others. Ask the member making the referral why this pastor might be good for Anytown Community Church. Ask former pastors and former members for referrals. Pastors may also get in touch directly in response to your announcements or advertisements or a referral from another source.

If you obtain names from regional or denominational offices, be prepared to supply their office staff with your completed church profile, so that they can make good recommendations. Once they have your church profile form, allow several weeks for the first round of names to be sent to you. Thereafter, depending on your polity, you might be able to call staff people directly with requests for new names.

Remember, the staff often works with many churches at the same time, so plan accordingly and be patient.

When names are received from sources other than your regional or denominational offices, contact the appropriate office to determine whether the pastor has a profile on file and request a copy. If a profile is not on file, you might write to the pastor directly or work through denominational channels. (For sample letters, see the section on "Sharing and Gathering Information" in chapter 8, "Connecting with Pastors".) If you receive the profile and it is out of date, write to the pastor and ask for an updated profile if he or she has an interest in further communication. It is difficult to get an accurate reading on a pastor or to make a decision about him or her if the profile is more than two years old.

As you move through the search, many pastors will be recommended to you or will contact you directly. If a pastor has been serving a congregation for only two or three years, do not put him or her on your list. You would not want a search committee to issue a call to *your* pastor after such a short time; therefore, respect this rule for all concerned. If you are affiliated with a denomination, you may find other policies or church-order rules that address how soon pastors may be approached for a new call.

Remember that not every pastor is interested in your church. Many pastors are happy in the ministries they have and will not entertain a call or even desire to receive information about your church. Respect their wishes.

Using the Web

Because of the power of the Web, if your church does not have a website, this is a good time to consider creating one. A website allows you to post photos, audio and video, and as much information about your church as you want to place there—including downloadable documents. Do not underestimate the number of pastors who are searching the Web to find a new pastoral call. (See chapter 3, "Using the Internet," for more information.)

The Pastoral Profile Form

A pastoral profile form is part of a church body's system that serves to match pastors to congregations. The profile form, usually managed by a denominational placement or vocations office, allows pastors to be introduced to churches that do not have a pastor or that soon will be without clergy leadership. Be forewarned that not all the pastors with forms on file are actually looking for a change in ministry.

The pastoral profile form is usually a several-page document with questions about a pastor's ministry and professional preferences, leadership and management style, and personal information. Its function is to provide search committees with enough information to determine whether a match between that pastor and the church may be possible. The form should be viewed as a screening aid to assist search committees in the first stage of their selection process. Review the forms, discussing them as a committee, to determine which pastors you want to know more about.

Each form typically begins with personal information: address, family information, number of years in the ministry, and present ministry location and number of years served there. Questions may focus on the pastor's ministry preferences, including the type of ministry setting (rural, suburban, or metropolitan), geographical areas, type of pastoral ministry, and congregation size desired.

Other questions will focus on professional preferences in preaching and teaching, pastoral calling, youth and elder ministry, counseling, evangelism, community involvement, and congregational focus. Special skills, languages, and continuing-education programs may also be listed.

Answers to the questions on the form may also describe the pastor's leadership and management style through the identification of specific qualities—for example, caring, effectiveness in administration, skill in relating to people, approachability, strength at taking initiative, and sensitivity to others' needs. (For a list of related qualities, see chapter 10, "Selection Criteria, Evaluation, and Recommendation.")

Pastors may also be asked to identify schools attended and degrees earned, relate personal and professional life stories, list published material, cite influences on their life and previous careers, and submit references.

What is typically not included in these forms is a history of the pastor's ministerial service. Take some time to inquire about where she has served in the past. Knowing where a pastor served, for how long, and the size of the church provides a larger picture of her pastoral service. This information may be available in denominational yearbooks or through your denomination office. If not, you can ask pastors to provide this important information. If you use this information to inquire about a pastor's service at a church, the best person to talk with is the lay chair of the church's board.

Creating Your Advertisement

Once you have completed your self-study and congregational survey and have written your church profile, try to describe your congregation in only a few sentences. This exercise is the first step in creating an advertisement for your church. Yours is only one church of many searching for a pastor. At any one time, many congregations are in some stage of the search process. Some denominations allow churches to advertise for a pastor; other do not. Remember that other churches are also advertising. Look through magazines and on the Web for current ads. Read and critique the following ads:

♦ ♦ ♦

Somewhere Church in Somewhere WA is seeking a new pastor. Please send inquiries to Search Committee, 123 Here Street, Somewhere, WA 98100.

♦ ♦ ♦

Due to the pending retirement of our pastor of 15 years, Hometown Church is looking for a pastor. Our church profile is available upon request. Contact the Search Committee, Hometown Church, 75 Center Road, Hometown, WA 98200.

◆ ◆ ◆

Midtown Church invites applications for the position of pastor to succeed Rev. G. Sermon, who is retiring. The Search Committee seeks a pastor with outstanding pulpit strength to present the gospel message effectively. This pastor should have good pastoral strength to relate to the needs of individual members. Strong administrative skills will help in leading a staff ministry and planning and coordinating worship. Progressive, visionary leadership will help our church fulfill its mission role in the broader community. Midtown Church has provided an effective, faithful ministry in a suburban setting for over fifty years. Resumes or inquiries should be sent to the Search Committee, 8910 Spirit Street, Midtown, MI 49500.

◆ ◆ ◆

Anytown Community Church, with 200 members and regular attendees, is now actively seeking a full-time pastor. Located on the East Side, Anytown and its surrounding communities are rich in cultural and ethnic diversity, which is reflected in the congregation, providing considerable potential for outreach and growth. The pastor should enjoy working in a decentralized church structure that is supported by a hardworking board, a Christ-centered staff, and active committees. Our worship services are celebratory, with a strong music and praise emphasis. If you feel God is leading you to this challenge, please send inquiry or profile to Mark Jordan, 12345 Alive Place, Anytown, CA 92100.

◆ ◆ ◆

Community Church in Walnut, IL is seeking a pastor. We're a suburban congregation of 75 families involved with Christian education and community activities. We seek a pastor committed to preaching and teaching who shares our vision for community service and outreach. Demonstrated leadership as a team builder and skills in reaching youth are also desirable. Please send inquiries or resumes to Search Committee, c/o Tim Lockley, 3232 Alpha Drive, Walnut, IL 61376.

◆ ◆ ◆

Your task is to create an ad that is honest, warm, and inviting to a pastor who is actively seeking a call to a new ministry, or who is on the edge of decision making. Did the first two ads catch your eye and make you want to write for more information? Most likely they did not. The third identifies the kind of pastor the church is looking for but tells little about the congregation. The fourth ad tells something about the area and possible opportunities, and a lot about the church, including its leadership and worship style. The fifth ad indicates something about the church and surrounding area, the congregation's focus, and specifies what the church is looking for in a pastor. The last two ads will generate more response than the first three ads. The last two ads also provide the name and address of a contact person. As appropriate, include phone and fax numbers, e-mail addresses, and the URL for your congregation's website.

Ask several committee members to write an ad, using the results of your congregational survey and information from your church profile form. Then use the best one or parts of several ads. Be creative but accurate. As a committee, talk the ad through word by word, thinking about what each word conveys. This is not the time to save a few dollars with a short ad that says little.

Running Your Ad

Review denominational, regional, and general religious publications to determine where to advertise. Call these publications and request a rate sheet, information about rates for repeat ads, and ad deadlines. The lead time to get an ad published may be several months. At any point in your search, you can rerun or modify the ad. In monthly magazines, because of the lead time, the same ad will typically run for several months. In weekly magazines, running the same ad every week for several months is costly, and you might get better responses by placing ads intermittently. Neither the readership nor the interest of pastors changes that much from week to week.

Don't forget to update your ad as necessary. If you indicate in the ad that you will have a church profile ready by a certain date, update the ad by that date. Failing to do so can indicate to readers that you have not received any responses to your initial ad, that you are out of touch with what your ad says, that you are not attentive to details, or that the search process might be difficult.

It is exciting to serve on a pastoral search committee and to see how many wonderful men and women God has prepared to lead the church. As you hear about them through your sources and read their profiles, you will be blessed. The next step is to make contact with the pastors.

CHART 7.1. Task Cluster: Finding Candidates

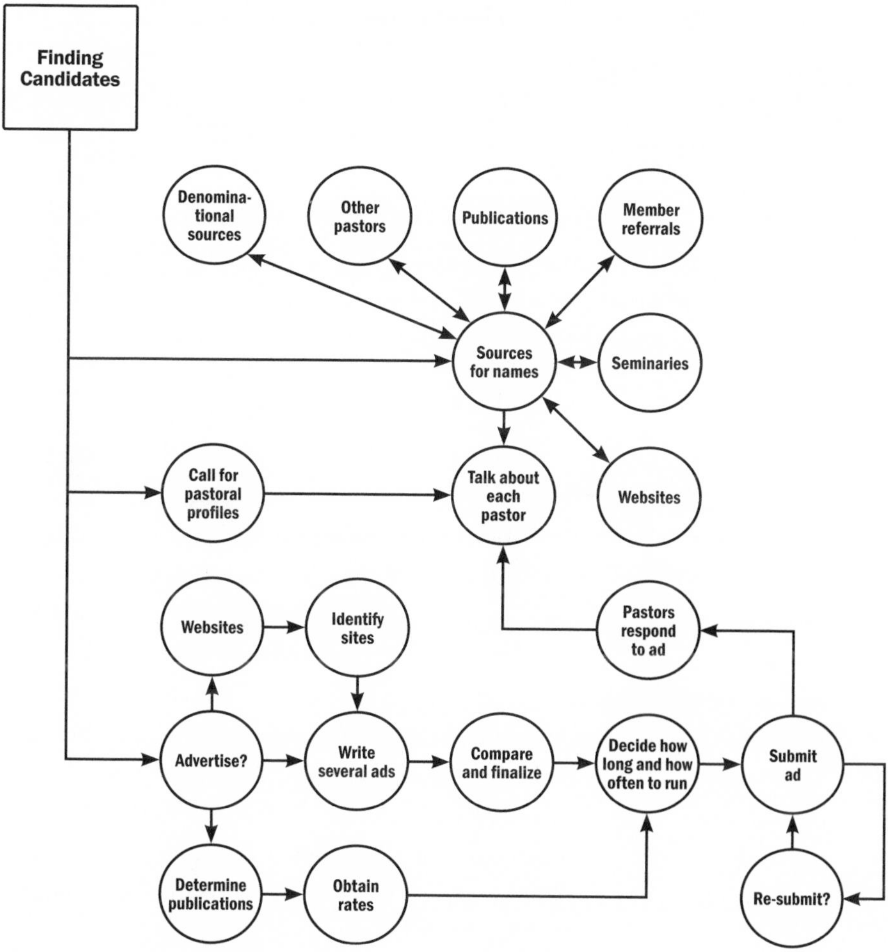

Chapter 8

◆ ◆ ◆

Connecting with Pastors

The search committee connects with pastors in many ways: face to face, over the phone, and through letters and e-mails. The quality of your communication with pastors throughout your search can make or break the effort. First impressions are important, but in every stage of the search process, pastors will be taking stock of how well you communicate and how you treat them. Most pastors know good communication. And, like congregations, they hate to be treated badly. Consider comments from several pastors about their experiences as you think about how you can communicate effectively:

- ◆ "They provided well-organized and ample materials, making regular, courteous, and caring calls to check on my progress."
- ◆ "They kept us informed of how the process was going, including my place in the process."
- ◆ "We need to cultivate more trust and respect for pastors."
- ◆ "Timing is important—it is difficult to be in a 'waiting mode' with one church when you need to make a decision on another church."
- ◆ "There is one thing that is usually in short supply on both sides, and that is honesty. Search committees should be willing to ask the hard questions."
- ◆ "They should have asked more questions of me in terms of my gifts, strengths, and weaknesses."

- ◆ "Give me their church profile first, and then ask me if I feel at all led to consider their ministry, rather than ask on the phone, throw my name into the hopper, and then send a profile."
- ◆ "A monthly letter should inform applicants of the search status. Few things are as frustrating as sending off an application and not hearing back for three months."

Communications

Stay on top of communications at all times. It takes an effort to present enough information to give pastors a clear, concise picture of your congregation's personality, where it has been, where it is going, its strengths and weaknesses, how its leadership functions, and what ministries it supports. Present a clear and honest picture in your ad, correspondence, church information packet and video; on your website, in interviews, and when hosting visiting pastors. Decide at the onset what tone your communications will take. Do you want to come across as formal and "all business," as warm and caring, or as a blend of the two?

In your pastoral search process, you may have contact with any number of pastors, from two to one hundred, depending on your process and the constraints of your denomination. And in the end, you will have rejected all but one! The way you communicate with these pastors, the quality of your search, and the respect you show are elements every search committee needs to keep in mind. Your search must provide positive care to all pastors with whom you connect. Every pastor should come away from your search process with good things to say about your church. A good exercise is to take a few minutes from time to time in your meetings to try to view the process from the pastors' perspective and through their eyes. Ask: "What would a pastor interested in our church think about . . . ?"

Treat each pastor as you would want to be treated, and you will be on your way to a positive relationship. Even if your congregation does not call the pastor, he or she will remember his or her experience with you. Pastors desire respect and courtesy, just as you and I do. Consider the following ways to show each candidate respect and courtesy.

These topics will be addressed in more detail as we move through the search process.

- ◆ Listen to him. Reflect back what he has said and ask questions about his answers if clarification is necessary.
- ◆ Tell him why you want him to serve your congregation.
- ◆ Give him an honest presentation about your church and its ministry, including problem areas.
- ◆ Do not judge him without giving an opportunity to respond.
- ◆ Realize that he may be serving a church or other organization that requires his time and attention, and that he cannot drop everything to complete a lengthy questionnaire or to attend a meeting on a moment's notice.
- ◆ Pick up his expenses, and manage the details when he comes for a visit.
- ◆ Include his spouse in the interviews and conference calls, at least for part of the time, and allow both to meet with the governing board when you talk about the life of your church.
- ◆ Focus on honesty, trust, and open communication.
- ◆ Be truthful. Do not "lead him on" or present false impressions about your church.

Be proactive, taking the initiative in making phone calls, supplying information before it is requested, and anticipating questions before they are asked. When initially making contact with each pastor, ask how he or she would like to communicate—by e-mail, phone, or a combination? Work hard to save pastors the expense and trouble of trying to reach someone on the committee. Decide how you will keep the pastors informed about your search process. Send out periodic updates by regular mail or e-mail, and make telephone calls to pastors in the advanced stages of the process, advising them where you are in the search process and how they fit into the picture. Let them know why you are still interested in them. Another medium for communicating with pastors is your church's website. Your webmaster could create a special webpage with information for pastors, and make that page accessible only to pastors and the search committee, perhaps by use of a secure password, or a nonpublic URL. This page might include photos, videos of groups and church activities, and audio—including interviews with members, staff, and the search committee.

The Pastor's Family

During the search process, an easily overlooked factor in communications is the pastor's spouse and children. Most pastors have spouses, who may have their own careers, and children with needs and school and sports interests. Consider the spouse in the materials you prepare, the way you present your church, and your written and telephone communications. Include him or her in any interviews. Seek out information on his or her gifts and ministries, but respect the spouse who does not desire an active role in the ministry of the church. Not all spouses are musically inclined, sing, lead Bible studies, and teach children. You may lose a qualified pastor if you do not include the spouse in the search process.

Moving from Stage to Stage

You will move through five stages as you work with pastors in the search process.
- *Stage I.* Sharing and Gathering Information
- *Stage II.* Pastoral Profile and Questionnaire
- *Stage III.* Sermon Tapes, Reference Checks, and Testing
- *Stage IV.* Interviews
- *Stage V.* Determining Whom to Recommend

You will need to decide how to move from stage to stage. Here are two options:
1.   You can choose to work with each pastor as he or she becomes known to you. This approach will result in your dealing with pastors at different stages at the same time. You may be preparing to interview four people, reviewing pastoral questionnaires from five, waiting for responses to eight church information packets, and deliberating about six inquiry letters. New pastors

can be introduced into the mix at any time. However, if you feel positive about a new person at a later point in your search, you will have to try to bring him or her without delay to the same stage as others who are already more familiar to you.

2.   You can study pastors' profiles as you receive them, screening a large selection of pastors before taking further action. Once a large number of profiles have been reviewed, move to the next stage, and then the next, narrowing the field as you go. Using this approach, you might review fifty profiles and narrow the field to ten for consideration. Unless you already know that all ten are open to a move, your list may easily be reduced to five or six.

Create a tracking system so you always know where a pastor is at any time in your search process. At each search committee meeting, members should be given an updated copy of the list, perhaps arranged in a chart. Mark new or changed entries with an asterisk or print them in bold, so that changes can be easily seen. A sample chart can be found at the end of this chapter.

At any stage, when either a pastor or the search committee decides not to continue the process, move the name and information to a *dropped* category in your tracking file. You will want to remember all the pastors with whom you have communicated, since some may indicate that they are open for reconsideration at a later date. Some pastors may find that their current church situations change, or that they are no longer talking with another church about a call, or they may have a change of heart and decide that they are open to beginning a dialogue with you about your church. Some pastors might ask to be removed from your list, concluding that they are not a good match for your church, or simply deciding to stay where they are now serving.

Stage I. Sharing and Gathering Information

Your initial contact is an inquiry. The pastor receives an inquiry letter or a phone call. Even though we live in an Internet world, do not make this initial contact via e-mail—it's too impersonal. The pastor is added to your tracking file at this point. If you review a pastor's profile received from your denomination and decide not to make personal contact, add the pastor's name to your tracking file anyway. That pastor may contact you on her own, and you need to know that she has already been reviewed. Keeping good records can save time for everyone.

Some pastors will not have profiles, or their profiles will be out of date. You might, if your denominational polity permits, contact some people directly. The first sample letter below, with a brochure of your church and a copy of your ad, may be used for an initial direct contact. If your letter of inquiry includes a date when a search committee member will call, be sure someone is assigned to make the call on the date given and follows through.

◆ ◆ ◆

Greetings from Anytown Community Church!

Anytown Community Church is seeking a pastor. You have been suggested as a possible candidate, and we would like to know if you are open to discussion about a call.

We are looking for a Spirit-filled man or woman who is excited about ministering to God's people and reaching out to the community. A copy of our recent advertisement is enclosed. We have prepared a comprehensive information package about our church and its ministries. If you are interested in hearing more about us, please submit a pastoral profile to our search committee for review. If our search committee members believe there is a possibility of a good match between you and us, we will send the information package to you.

A committee member will be calling you on _____ *[insert a date ten days from the anticipated receipt of the letter]* to inquire about your interest in Anytown Community Church.

We are looking forward to talking with you.

◆ ◆ ◆

The sample letter says the committee members will review the submitted pastoral profile and will send an information packet if they believe the person might be a good fit for the congregation. The search committee may decide, however, to send packets to all pastors who express an interest, whether in response to an ad or a letter from the congregation, or at the pastor's own initiative. Record the date the packet is sent, and follow up with a phone call *on the date promised* to answer any questions and to determine whether further communications are warranted.

If the pastor is open to further consideration, he or she should be encouraged to complete and return your pastoral questionnaire. If you do not have a copy of his or her pastoral profile, request a copy.

Stage II. Pastoral Profile and Questionnaire

Once the pastoral profile and questionnaire are received, make copies for the search committee members to review before your next meeting. The pastoral profile is discussed in chapter 7, "Finding Candidates." A sample pastoral questionnaire is found in appendix D.

You can learn much about a candidate from a pastoral profile. The form will provide information about a pastor's personal history, his or her ministry and professional preferences, and leadership and management style. This information will help you understand who the pastor is and what type of ministry he or she is seeking. You may be interested in a pastor but find that she is interested in a rural ministry—and yours is a metropolitan inner-city ministry. Your church may have a vibrant youth and singles ministry, but a possible candidate may signal that he does not work well with youth. These two pastors would likely be eliminated from your list. On the other hand, a pastor who indicates an interest in outreach might do well in your church if you have a thriving evangelistic ministry.

The pastoral questionnaire will provide the search committee with insights beyond what the pastoral profile shows. You can ask questions you consider relevant to your church and explore the pastor's thinking about leadership, administration, worship, education, evangelism, and fellowship. Each pastor should complete the same questionnaire. The sample questionnaire was developed after consultation with pastors. It is nonthreatening and simply asks for a response to key words or phrases, allowing the pastor to complete it quickly. You will receive concise statements in response. If you have identified styles or issues that are important to your church and if you need to know each pastor's views about them, add the relevant questions to your questionnaire. Each pastor's response will be matched against what you determine to be appropriate for your church and ministry. Whether you use this questionnaire, modify it for your church's needs, or use another, remember that the pastor probably is now in ministry to a church or other organization and cannot spend hours completing a long form. If your denomination has a pastoral profile form, your questionnaire should avoid questions on the same topics. Offer to send the questionnaire by e-mail as a Word document so that pastors do not need to complete the form by hand. You might also make the form available for downloading on the "pastoral search" page on your website.

As the search committee discusses the pastoral profile and questionnaire, its members should be aware of what will affect their decisions. Chapter 10, "Selection Criteria, Evaluation, and Recommendation," provides guidelines on establishing a method of assessing pastoral candidates.

Stage III. Sermon Tapes, Reference Checks, and Testing

With a positive decision on the questionnaire and profile, several steps can now be taken at the same time. Sermon tapes, CDs, or DVDs are valuable instruments in the search process and can help committee members connect with the pastor. A sermon without the context of a complete service is harder to evaluate, however, so consider requesting recordings of one or two complete recent services. If the pastor's church does not record services, ask if an exception can be made. While audio is good, videos have advantages, since they allow you to observe the pastor as worship leader and to get a better feel for the flow of the service, as well as for the pastor's preaching abilities.

When the tape, CD, or DVD is received, make a copy for each member of the search committee. A sermon on audiotape or CD can be evaluated for biblical content, application, challenge, delivery, humor, illustrations, and length; and a worship service can be evaluated for flow, tone, and spirit, as well as for the quality of the prayers. In addition to those criteria, a DVD allows you to appraise the pastor's charisma, eye contact, comfort level, mannerisms, movement, personality, and appearance. Talk about the recordings as a committee, first sharing your individual views and then developing a group assessment. Review "The Importance of Preaching" in chapter 10, "Selection Criteria, Evaluation, and Recommendation," for more specifics on evaluating preaching and the worship service.

Decide whether the search committee budget allows travel for one or more committee members to attend a service at the pastor's congregation. Some committees believe that the benefits of observing a worship service far outweigh the expense, so attending a service conducted by a pastoral candidate is recommended. If you plan to observe a Sunday service, decide beforehand whether you will let the pastor know that you will be there. You must respect her current ministry and not tell anyone why you are there. Be a fly on the wall, simply a visitor. Whoever goes to hear the pastor then reports on his or her impressions to the full committee.

While waiting for the recordings, begin your reference checks. If you choose to do personality testing, that process needs to start. See chapter 9, "Managing References, Testing, Interviews, and Red Flags," for guidelines on these processes. If the search committee feels good about continuing after the checks have been completed, move to the next stage.

Stage IV. Interviews

Now it's time to contact the pastor to arrange an interview. If he or she is close by, the interview can be conducted face to face. If the distance is great, arrange for an interview via a telephone conference call or a webcam-equipped computer. Let the pastor know when the search committee meets, and ask whether he or she can be available, but plan to work your interview around his or her schedule. See "The Interview" in chapter 9, "Managing References, Testing, Interviews, and

Red Flags," for guidelines on interviewing. The interview is usually the first opportunity for the entire team to talk with the pastor. You know her from her profile and questionnaire, and she knows you from your church information packet and your website. An interview allows you to get to know each other at a deeper level.

Stage V. Determining Whom to Recommend

As pastoral profiles are read, reference checks made, tapes reviewed, and interviews completed, the field narrows. See chapter 10, "Selection Criteria, Evaluation, and Recommendation," for guidelines on this part of the process.

This phase can be difficult. The committee should talk candidly about each pastor and his or her potential fit for your church's strengths and weaknesses, personality, ministries, vision, and mission. Allow each member to speak without interruption about each pastor considered. Doubts must be shared within the committee and openly discussed. Whether you vote formally or simply come to an agreement, there should be an understanding among the committee members that the decision about each pastor is right for your church. Following this discussion, rank your top two or three choices and move forward with the invitations for each of the pastors to come for a weekend with your congregation.

The decision about how many pastors to recommend should be made early in the search process. In some churches, the search committee chooses the candidate and recommends that person to the board and the congregation for a call. Other committees select two pastors and present them both for the congregation to consider. Whether to present one, two, or even more is a matter of the number of pastors you have to work with, the choices of the search committee, and your denomination's church order or policies. Two pastors are simpler than three for both the search committee and the congregation to deal with. If three pastors visit, the first pastor may not receive as fair an evaluation as the third, simply because people will most easily remember the last person. Considering a third pastor may also make it more difficult to reach consensus about which one to call. See chapter 12, "Managing the Call Process," for guidelines on this part of the process.

If you receive an inquiry from a pastor no longer under consideration, send a letter explaining why he or she was removed from consideration. The sample letter below may be used as a guide. You do not need to keep your denominational or regional offices informed about your decisions unless they require it.

◆ ◆ ◆

Our Pastoral Search Committee would like to thank you for your interest in Anytown Community Church. We appreciate your response to our ad.

Much of our initial process has been to reflect on our past, identify our strengths and weaknesses, and assess our vision and goals. In this process, we have determined specific pastoral gifts areas we believe are needed to guide our church at this time. We have considered many qualified pastors. After comparing your profile and questionnaire with our church's profile, and praying for direction, we believe you and Anytown Community Church would not be a good match.

Your profile reflects experiences and gifts that we know will be a benefit to a church that matches your profile. As we pray for God's guidance in our search process, we also will pray for his blessings on your present and future ministry.

◆ ◆ ◆

Tracking Pastors

The secretary of the search committee should track contacts and actions related to each pastor. The easiest method is to attach a list of steps to each pastor's profile. It is better to be too thorough than to miss an important contact or event. Dates can be added to the list as steps are completed.

Inquiry letter sent   _____

Inquiry letter sent   _____

Interest (yes/no/maybe later)   _____

Church information packet sent   _____

Follow-up call made   _____

Pastoral profile received: current (yes/no)   _____

New profile requested   _____

Profile received   _____

Pastoral profile reviewed   _____

Questionnaire received   _____

Questionnaire reviewed   _____

Sermon tape or videos requested   _____

Sermon tape or video reviewed   _____

References checked   _____

Testing completed/reviewed   _____

Telephone interview completed   _____

Status:

    Advance to final stage   _____

    Do not pursue   _____

    Notification of decision sent   _____

    Church packet returned   _____

It is also helpful for the search committee to know the status of each prospective candidate. The sample chart below provides that kind of tracking. Note the dates when the initial inquiry is made, when profiles and questionnaires are received, tapes received, reference checks made, testing reviewed, and the interview completed. Move the names from section to section as they progress though the process. Be sure to move the dropped names to the last section, so that you have a record showing all pastors with whom you have talked. Some pastors may indicate an openness to further discussion at a later date if you are still in the search process. When a pastor's status changes to "not available" or "dropped," remove the profile from your binder, but retain all profiles until the search process is completed.

CHART 8.1. Prospective Candidates

Pastor Number	Church location	Inquiry (I) Packet (P) Both (B)	Profile (P) Quest (Q) Both (B)	Sermon tape reviewed	References checked	Testing done	Interview completed
Stage V. Determining Whom to Recommend							
Pastor 4	Orange, CA	9-21 (B)	9-28 (B)	10-20	11-12	11-28	12-16
Pastor 11	Ames, IA	10-22 (B)	10-29 (B)	11-15	11-20	12-6	12-14
Stage IV. Interviews							
Pastor 8	Trenton, NJ	10-16 (B)	10-30 (B)	11-16	11-24	12-2	12-14
Pastor 9	Wichita, KS	10-20 (B)	11-8 (B)	11-20	11-26	12-8	12-16
Stage III. Sermon Tapes, Reference Checks, and Testing							
Pastor 3	Buffalo, NY	9-26 (B)	10-8 (B)	10-29	11-16		
Pastor 7	Prescott, AZ	10-6 (B)	11-2 (B)	11-26			
Stage II. Pastoral Profile and Questionnaire							
Pastor 5	Pueblo, CO	9-29 (B)	10-26 (Q)				
Pastor 10	Bend, OR	10-18 (B)	11-13 (P)				
Stage I. Sharing and Information Gathering							
Pastor 2	Marion, GA	9-26 (P)					
Pastor 13	Reno, NV	11-16 (I)					
Pastor 14	Mpls. MN	12-10 (I)					
Dropped							
Pastor 1	Atlanta, GA	9-10	9-15				Not a match
Pastor 6	Seattle, WA	9-29	10-20	11-6			Not a match
Pastor 12	York, PA						No interest

Use this chart as a guide for developing your own tracking system. Make yours as simple or complex as needed to keep your search committee updated on the status of each pastor in the process. The chart can easily be created in Word or Excel.

Communication is a large part of your search. At every point in the process, you will communicate in some way with pastors. You need

CHART 8.2. Task Cluster: Communications with Pastors

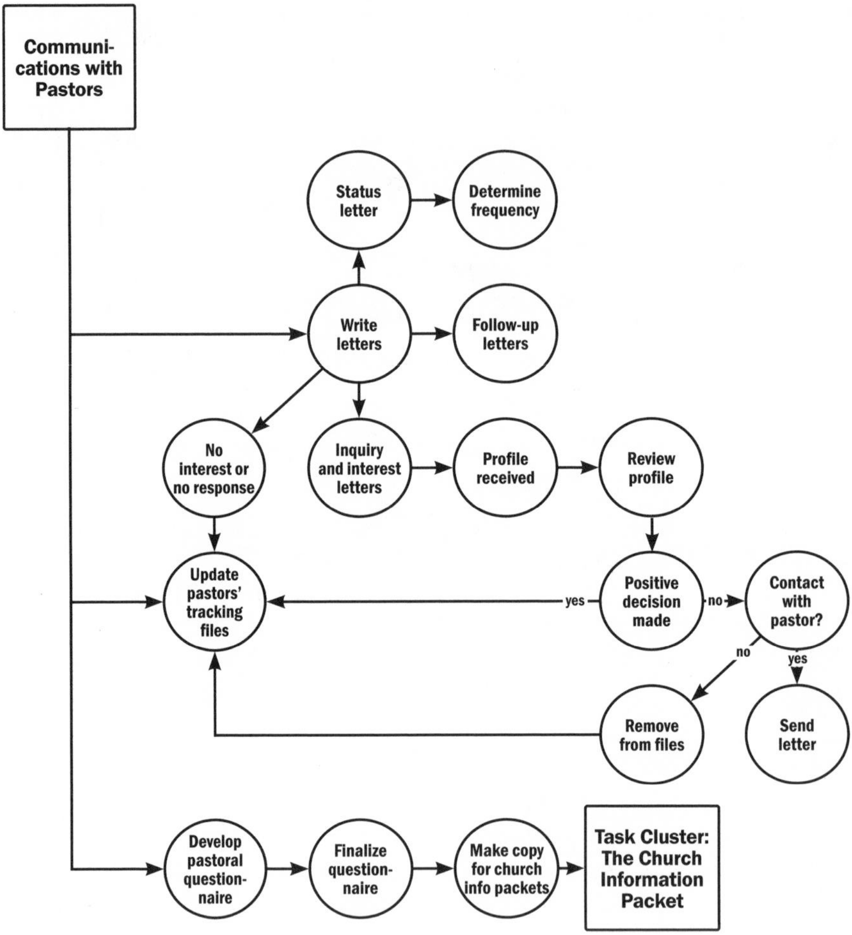

to do it well. As you move forward, you will be working on several aspects of the process at the same time. You will be managing references, testing, interviews, and red flags, discussed in chapter 9. Also review chapter 10, "Selection Criteria, Evaluation, and Recommendation," for tips on how to assess each pastor. Some of the committee should be looking at chapter 11, "Presenting Your Best Side," while others are beginning to study how to manage the call process, chapter 12. The process may sound overwhelming, but when you understand all the pieces of the puzzle, the picture will become clear.

CHART 8.3. Task Cluster: Moving from Stage to Stage

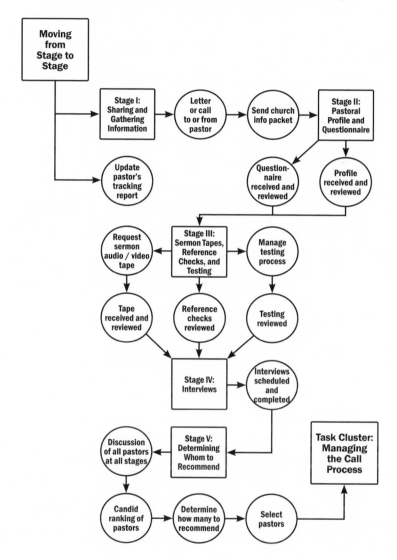

Chapter 9

◆ ◆ ◆

Managing References, Testing, Interviews, and Red Flags

The pastoral profile forms you receive from your denominational or regional offices or from the pastor should provide three or more references. These may be pastors or laypeople. They are individuals whom search committees may ask about a pastor's abilities and gifts for ministry. Let the pastor know that you will be checking references, and get his approval before contacting anyone from his current church or organization. Violating this guideline will result in the pastor's loss of confidence in your process and may cause problems in his current setting.

Prepare a list of open-ended questions before making the phone call. Again, emphasize that the information will be kept in confidence. Below are sample questions:

- How long have you known the pastor?
- What ministry relationships have you had with her?
- Can you state her pastoral vision?
- How does she lead the congregation?
- How does she promote and develop personal growth in her ministry?
- How does she challenge the congregation?
- How effective has her ministry been?
- Has the church grown, and have new ministries been started?

- ◆ Please describe the area of ministry that you believe to be her greatest strength.
- ◆ What are her weaknesses as a pastor?
- ◆ How would you assess her credibility?
- ◆ How well does she relate to the congregation and how well do the members relate to her?
- ◆ How strong are her administrative skills?
- ◆ Have there been any troubling problems during her ministry, and if so, have they been resolved?
- ◆ Does she work well with other ministry staff members and employees of the church?
- ◆ Do you have any other candid and confidential comments to share?

You should feel comfortable calling the individuals listed as references and asking questions. It works best to have one search committee member make calls to all the references for one pastor. When you call, identify yourself, your church, and the purpose of the call. Ask the person called if the time is convenient and if he or she has ten to fifteen minutes to answer a few questions about pastor X. If not, make an appointment for another time. Explain that you are interested in short, concise statements. Remember to take into consideration the time zones if calling outside your area. Do not ask for a callback if the person is out; you are responsible for the expense of the call. Take notes during or immediately after the call. Remember that you are responsible for giving the full search committee a report on the calls.

Be candid in your conversation. If you sense hesitance, ask for clarification. Emphasize that all comments will be kept in confidence and shared only with the search committee. At the end of each call, ask for any final thoughts the reference would like to share. Finally, thank each person for his or her assistance. If several of the references are not available when you try to make contact, request others from the pastor.

As references are checked, the search committee may sense an issue that needs additional explanation. You may want to call the person with whom you first spoke. You might also speak with other references, pastors in the region or denomination, or even the pastor herself to clarify the question. Do your best to resolve the issue.

The Web is powerful, and it is easy to use Google or another search engine to do a search of any pastor you are considering. Simply type the pastor's name in the search box. It may take a bit of effort to look through the results to determine if any refer to your candidate, but one member of the search committee can easily do this research. The Web search can be modified by adding the names of cities or churches where the pastor has previously served. If the search results seem confusing, check the search engine website you are using to learn how to do advanced searches.

Some churches will require a criminal background check and/ or a credit check. If your board or church attorney suggests this step as part of the search process, be sure to advise any potential pastoral candidates of this requirement. Several companies that conduct background checks and screenings for churches are listed in appendix A, "Pastoral Search Resources." You will need the pastor's Social Security number or other personal information and possibly a signed release to obtain these checks. Be sure that you are clear about what checks are included. Most states review only their own records. For a more comprehensive check, you will need to request an FBI check, too.

Using Test Instruments

One way to determine whether a pastor would be a good match for your church is to use one of the many test instruments available through a Christian counselor or a Christian management consultant. This form of testing has become standard in religious organizations, including churches, across the country. Common tests include the Taylor-Johnson Temperament Analysis and the Myers-Briggs Type Indicator, but the counselor may recommend others. Each test is different, but generally the tests identify personality styles, temperaments, and communication and relationship skills. The tests can effectively identify ways the pastor and the church match. The use of two tests is recommended as a check and balance. The management of the tests by an experienced counselor is important. Do not pick a test simply because you have heard of it. Choose a test based on the recommendations of the counselor only after meeting with him or her. The counselor's knowledge of the testing instrument and how to score and interpret it is the key to the tests' value for the search process. Try not to select tests that take more than one hour to complete.

Look in the Yellow Pages under "counselors" or "marriage, family, child and individual counselors." You may also search the Web for these terms followed by your city's name. Your first preference should naturally be a Christian counselor, but be aware that not all counselors who are committed Christians identify themselves as such. Ask pastors from neighboring churches or denominational or regional judicatory staff members for the names of counselors with whom they have worked. Call several counselors, and ask whether they do psychological testing and evaluation, and whether they have experience using tests in pastoral searches. Then invite one to come and talk to your search committee. This meeting is an important starting point for the counselor. Ask if there will be an additional fee for this session. Information you provide about your church and its staff, board, and members will help the counselor understand the congregation. He or she needs to know the kind of leader you are looking for, the characteristics sought, and something about your church. You may be asked about your previous pastor. When a counselor knows what you hope to gain through testing, appropriate test instruments can be recommended. If there is no Christian counselor in your area, the process can be done via mail and conference calls between the search committee and the counselor. Be sure to ask about costs for the test instruments and written summaries. Costs will vary depending on the number and types of tests used. Factor these costs into your search budget.

The testing process is intended to determine why one pastor would be a better match for your church than another pastor. Your search committee is called to discover the pastor that God would have serve your church. The counselor will provide the search committee and each pastor tested with a written summary of the test results. The pastor and search committee should receive the same summary, which should address the matter of an appropriate match for the pastor and the church, not point out deficiencies or problem areas.

The sample letter below can be used to introduce the testing process to the pastor. Not all pastors will be open to your using these tests. Some may even elect not to complete the tests, but the majority will appreciate the opportunity to find out more about themselves. In fairness, if you decide to use testing, all candidates should have to complete the tests to be considered. You need to decide at what point in the search to conduct the tests. Try to schedule them after you have narrowed the candidate list to one or two, but before the candidates' visits, in case questions surface.

◆ ◆ ◆

Our pastoral search committee is moving forward in our search process, and we are excited about the men and women with whom we are in conversation. We have been in touch with the references provided, have listened to worship tapes, and are moving into the next stages of the process.

As we stated in an earlier phone call, we have arranged with Christian Counseling Center, Inc. (CCC) to send one test to all pastors we are considering. The Taylor-Johnson Temperament Analysis focuses on general personality characteristics to identify a match with our style and ministry requirements. The test instrument will be administered by Bill Fielding of CCC, who will send the test with an explanatory cover letter, score it, and give us a summary of findings that he believes will assist us in our search process. He will also send you the same summary of findings. He alone will see and handle the test, so your confidentiality will be protected. You should receive the material in a few days. We realize that time is valuable, but we would appreciate your completing the test in the coming week.

Most churches today use some form of testing in their search process. Many seminaries also use tests with new students, and specialized ministry areas often require testing. We selected a test that we believe will not be too time-consuming or threatening, and we are confident that this test can help us both be assured of a good match.

We have heard good things about you as a pastor and pray for God's best for you in your ministry search. Should you have any questions about Anytown Community Church, our ministries, or our search process, please call.

◆ ◆ ◆

The testing process is a subject that should be kept confidential between the search committee and the pastors. There is no need for the congregation to know about it.

The Interview

The interview provides an opportunity for direct conversation between the full search committee and the pastor being considered. This may be face to face, by telephone, or via the Web. A face-to-face interview is always the first choice but may not be practical. Telephone interviews are best done with a speakerphone, so that everyone can hear both sides of the conversation. If you do not have access to a telephone with a speakerphone unit, one can be purchased for about thirty dollars. Consider taping the calls, with the permission of the pastor, so that the committee can listen to calls when the process is further along.

The Web is a great alternative, even better than a speakerphone, because it allows video. Skype *(skype.com)* is a free, Web-based software application you download and use to make free calls over the Internet. If each party has access to a computer camera, Skype transmits both voice and video, which means that your search committee and the pastor being interviewed can hear and see each other in real time. The search committee and pastor each sit facing a webcam-equipped computer. You can search the Web for other, similar services. Be sure to make a test call before the day of the interview. If you expect the pastor to see the full committee, you will have to check camera angles and coverage distances for your computer's camera.

The search committee chair should call the pastor and arrange an interview at a time convenient for all parties. Let the pastor know how much time to block out for the interview and what time you will call. If the pastor is married, invite his or her spouse to join in a portion of the conversation. When scheduling two calls on the same evening, allow time to review the first interview before moving to the second. The entire search committee should be present for all interviews. When scheduling interviews in different parts of the country, pay attention to time-zone differences. Allow at least forty-five minutes for the call. All committee members should review copies of the pastor's profile and pastoral questionnaire beforehand.

Before the call is made, each committee member should think of questions that he or she would like to ask. Rather than asking open-ended questions about hypothetical situations, ask how the pastor has handled ministries and issues in the past. Past behaviors are the best indicator of future behaviors. Develop a single list of questions so that each pastor is asked about the same topics. Depending on each pastor's profile and answers to his or her questionnaire, you might have several additional personal questions for each pastor. Decide who will start the call, make introductions, and ask the first questions. Watch your time closely. One person should be in charge of the conversation. Let each committee member ask at least two questions. A list of potential questions is included below, followed by some possible quetsions from the pastor that the committee should be prepared to answer. Develop more questions based on the pastor's profile and pastoral question-naire, your church structure, and your strengths and weaknesses:

- What is your passion?
- Tell us about your spiritual walk.
- Tell us about your call to ministry.
- How do you achieve personal growth in your ministry?
- How have you challenged your congregation?
- What style of worship do you enjoy?
- What expectations of your board have you had?
- What situations frustrate you the most?
- How have you handled disagreements?
- Describe your greatest strengths and abilities.
- What are your greatest weaknesses?
- How do you handle leadership training?
- When facing a problem, what questions do you naturally ask?
- How would you describe your leadership style?
- Explain your style of counseling.
- How will you know God's will in this matter?

In preparing for the interview, remember that you will be asked questions also. Below are several possible questions pastors may ask.

- Why are you interested in me as a pastor?
- What role do you expect my family to play in your church?
- What concerns need to be addressed in the congregation and the community?
- What significant events and people have shaped your church, and how?
- What is your vision for your congregation?

It is important to know what you cannot ask. These include questions about age, physical characteristics, disabilities or chronic illnesses, and national origin. You may already have this information in the pastor's profile, but only if he or she has voluntarily added it. The pastor may mention it in an interview, but federal laws govern what cannot be asked of any candidate. Your supervisor or judicatory can help with interview do's and don'ts.

Allow time for the pastor to ask any final questions. Before ending the call, let him or her know what happens next and when you will make contact. Committee members should take notes during and after the call, recording enough information about the call to be able to reflect on the interview later when the field is being narrowed. Each member should note significant impressions.

Sometimes, after the initial interview, the committee will decide to do another round of interviews. Generally, the final two or three candidates are invited for a second interview. The prayer is that out of these finalists, one or two will be selected to come for a visit—and a possible call.

Dealing with Red Flags

As you read pastors' profiles and pastoral questionnaires, listen to their sermon tapes, interview them, or talk to their references, there may be pastors about whom search committee members feel some uncertainty. Call these uncertainties *red flags* and allow them to be discussed in your meetings.

It is wise to understand from the start that not every pastor will be a good match for your church, and some pastors will not seem right because of these red flags. Each member of the search committee has the obligation to raise to the committee any red-flag issues he or she might sense.

Red flags may take many forms. A red flag may be as simple as a strong feeling that several search committee members have about a pastor. One may arise because her views on a topic are different from that of the majority of your church membership. You may sense that he will not relate well to an age group that is a priority in your church. Red flags may also concern worship style, sermon delivery, or even a control issue.

The committee needs to discuss the issue and find answers to its questions. That may mean talking to the pastor or his references, asking for more references, talking to another pastor in the region where the pastor is serving, or simply talking as a committee. Remember that there are two sides to every issue, so take the time to respectfully explore both sides. Whatever the issue, the search committee needs to talk it through, perhaps do some research, and decide how to proceed. If the red flag is one about relationships, probe deeply, talking with people who can address your questions. Some red flags will end a relationship. If this is the case and you have been in conversation with the pastor, a letter or phone call should be made soon to let the pastor know the committee has decided he or she is not a good match for the congregation.

The process of checking references, testing, conducting interviews, and dealing with red flags can be time-consuming. Whether you are working with three pastors or six pastors in this phase of the search, you will be busy with phone calls to make and reports to read. Your search is narrowing. The rewards will be great as you continue in the search and determine your selection criteria, evaluate each pastor, and, finally, make a recommendation.

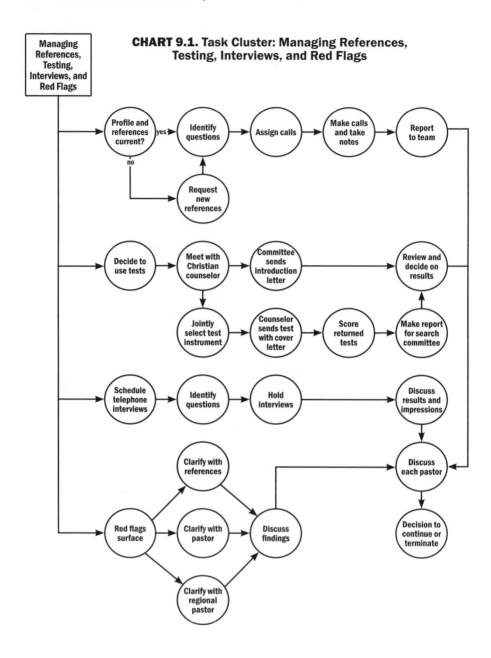

CHART 9.1. Task Cluster: Managing References, Testing, Interviews, and Red Flags

Chapter 10

◆ ◆ ◆

Selection Criteria, Evaluation, and Recommendation

It is important to determine the selection criteria for your pastoral search. Without this step, you will not know how to evaluate each pastor. A good starting point is to talk about your vision of a new pastor. Each member of your search committee will have a vision of the kind of person your next pastor should be, as well as what he or she should not be. You already know how your church looks. Now, how would it look with a new pastor? Spend time as a search committee talking about this prospect. What is your vision of your church under new leadership? What skills and professional qualities would you like your new pastor to have? What types of experience or education are important?

A second step is to identify specific attributes that you would find valuable in a new pastor. Below is a list of possibilities. Use this list, add to it, or develop your own. Narrow your list to the top twelve to fifteen attributes that you as a committee agree you want to find in your next pastor. Then sort them into two categories: *essential* and *desirable*. Remember these attributes as you talk about each candidate. The list can be an important resource to share with a Christian counselor if you decide to use personality tests.

CHART 10.1. Qualities of a Pastor

Able to delegate	Analytical	Approachable	Articulate
Assertive	Caring	Committed	Creative
Decisive	Dedicated	Determined	Diligent
Diplomatic	Disciplined	Discreet	Effective
Empathic	Energetic	Enthusiastic	Flexible
Forgiving	Friendly	Gospel-centered	Honest
Humble	Humorous	Imaginative	Innovative
Insightful	Intelligent	Intuitive	Loyal
Mature	Organized	Perceptive	Persistent
Personable	Persuasive	Positive	Precise
Professional	Progressive	Reliable	Responsible
Results-oriented	Self-assured	Sensitive	Stable
Strong	Studious	Supportive	Tactful
Tolerant	Trustworthy	Wise	Administrator
Communicator	Facilitator	Goal setter	Negotiator
Person of integrity	Planner	Preacher	Problem solver
Team player	Traditionalist	Trainer	Unifier

As you read pastors' profiles and pastoral questionnaires, and talk with the pastors and their references, use your intuition to determine whether the pastor has the attributes you selected.

The third step is to review your completed congregational survey. (See "Creating Your Congregational Survey" in chapter 6 and the sample survey in appendix C.) What has the congregation identified as the important professional qualities and expectations of the next pastor? Some specific items are preaching, administration, leadership, counseling, and program development. How does the congregation view strengths, weaknesses, needs, and interests? Specific items include ministries to youth or seniors, community outreach, education, family ministries, worship services, and discipleship. The results of your survey will tell you how the congregation thinks about key pastoral and congregational areas. If you have recently completed strategic planning or a master plan of your church, review that document for similar information.

Weighing Selection Criteria

Did the congregation identify some of the desired professional qualities that the search committee singled out? Did the results of the survey match what the search committee thought were the congregational strengths, weaknesses, and needs? How do these three areas fit with the vision the search committee has of your new pastor? What pastoral skills and background are necessary to work well with the three areas? Did anything surprise you in the survey results? Talk about these questions to finalize your selection criteria.

Having identified what you are looking for in your next pastor, list the criteria by three categories: preferred skills and background, desired personal attributes, and areas of congregational focus. Keep your list as concise as possible. When the list is complete, talk about it as a committee. Which factors are the most important? Which are secondary? Decide how to weigh each criterion. The simplest method is to rank them from high to low. Another option is to assign a percentage number to each criterion—with the total equaling 100 percent. Each pastor should be evaluated against all your selection criteria. Determine the minimum acceptable criteria.

A thorough knowledge of your selection criteria can help you in reviewing and discussing pastoral questionnaires and in participating in interviews. As you read pastors' questionnaires, listen to their worship tapes, and interview them, you will be better able to relate their experiences, skills, and personal qualities to what you have identified as important selection criteria. Using your intuition is valuable in the selection process, and an established set of selection criteria will help you feel comfortable with your intuition. (In fact, intuition and "chemistry" may be the deciding factors: "These guys are both highly qualified and meet our criteria, but we're excited about this one and feel as though we've known him all our lives, while we feel kind of blah about the other one.")

It is easy to get hung up on whom you want as your next pastor rather than on whom you need. These are two distinct areas. "Wants" are things you would like to have. "Needs" are what you must have. As you have worked through the process of determining who you are as a church and creating your church information packet, some areas may have risen to a more important level than others. Possible areas include a focus on small groups, pastoral care, teaching, missions, training for specific ministries, or another area. Hopefully, you will know whether these are wants or needs.

Determine how your next pastor fits with your church's focus. For example, missions may be a key focus for your church, but does that mean your next pastor must be gifted in this area? Are there other staff or members who can take the lead in missions, or who already have? Remember that your next pastor should have gifts to best match your selection criteria and the church's focus.

The Importance of Preaching and Leading Worship

The search committee members will want to talk about the importance of preaching and leading worship and determine how they will rank this element in relation to other selection criteria. The decision to consider a pastor should not be based on preaching alone but should take into account other professional skills and gifts. Administration, leadership, planning and vision setting, team building, and other areas of ministry are important. However, preaching and leading worship tend to become a deciding factor.

Whatever professional skills and gifts you determine to be your selection criteria, a basic fact remains: if the preaching is weak, the church may suffer. The congregation sees and hears more of a pastor in the pulpit than in any other role. He may be the best administrator in the world, but if his preaching is dull or the messages weak, other areas of ministry will suffer. This is truer in one-pastor churches than in churches where other staff may share in the preaching and other ministry areas. It's also truer in churches that have sermon-centered worship than in liturgical churches that have Holy Communion as the center of worship every Sunday and are accustomed to hearing a brief homily from the clergy leader rather than a full-blown, pull-out-all-the-stops sermon. Talk as a committee about how the church can grow with good preaching and about how lives will be changed and members challenged as God's Word lives in them. But be careful that your expectations about the results of the pastor's preaching are realistic.

How can the search committee identify good preaching? All members will have preconceived ideas about what constitutes good preaching—ideas based on their own experiences. It is helpful for the committee to talk about and understand generally accepted criteria for good preaching. Elizabeth Achtemeier, in her short book *So You're Looking For a New Preacher* (Grand Rapids: Eerdmans, 1991), distills her wisdom learned as an adjunct professor of Bible and homiletics. She states, "In short, good preaching leads you into a new or renewed experience of the work of God in your life and in the life of your congregation. Good preaching opens the way for God's action and God's changes to be wrought in human hearts and lives" (p. 24). She then talks about understanding preaching and worship:

- Weigh the message against the Word. Is the pastor's message from the Word and illuminated by Scripture?
- Do the illustrations and language make the message clear?
- Are we reminded that God is active here and now in our lives?
- Is the structure of the message logical? Can you trace its argument?
- Does the message hold your interest to its end and appeal to your heart as well as your mind?
- Are the prayers, music, and other parts of the liturgy connected with the message?
- Are the prayers to God or to the congregation? Do they express sincere offerings of heartfelt praise and confession, petition, and gratitude?
- Do the message and the delivery carry a sense of energy?
- Does the pastor seem to be worshiping with the congregation?
- What attitude is conveyed by the pastor's delivery, his voice, gestures, and body language?

Achtemeier also recommends learning about the pastor's personal life and growth areas:

- ◆ Ask how she is growing in her understanding of Scripture. What are her disciplines of Bible study and prayer?
- ◆ Ask about her study habits. What theology books has she read in the past three months?
- ◆ Ask about her reading of good literature. What fiction, poetry, or other literature has she read recently that has contributed to her imagination, creativity, and style of speech?
- ◆ Ask about her other interests. How does she use her leisure time?
- ◆ Ask about her commitment to continuing education. What would she do with five to ten days of study leave each year?

The Evaluation Process

From the initial contact with each pastor, you will be in an evaluation mode. The first collection of information you see about most pastors will be either their pastoral profiles or their pastoral questionnaires. As you read and discuss these in your meetings, you will need to decide whether to move forward in the process with each pastor. In some cases the answer will be clear to all committee members, while at other times you will talk quite a while before coming to an agreement. You may also decide to continue to the next stage in the process to gain additional information before making a decision.

You now have a lot of material on which to base your decision. From the pastoral profile, you moved to a completed pastoral questionnaire. From the pastoral questionnaire, you moved to the calls made to the references, then to the worship tape and sermon, and finally to the personal interview. If you have talked to other pastors or denominational representatives, take their views into account.

As you talk about each of these factors, pieces of the puzzle will fit together. The information you receive about each pastor will serve to build a picture in each of your minds about him or her. Discuss each pastor candidly:

- How does he or she rank against your selection criteria?
- How do you rate the preaching and worship?
- What were the comments from the references?
- Do the test instruments suggest a good match?
- Did the pastor's answers on the pastoral questionnaire help you understand him or her and seem to indicate that this person brings what your church needs?
- What were your impressions from the personal interview?
- How well do you think the pastor will work with other staff, and vice versa?

In the early stages of the search process, you evaluated pastors on the basis of information they provided. As you narrow the field, your evaluations of the remaining pastors will become more focused. Ask one another, "If we were to choose now, whom would we choose and why?" Some members may have insights that others miss. You will be surprised at how often you find that you are not far apart on your thoughts. Committee members should review "Task Cluster: Moving from Stage to Stage" at the end of chapter 9 if they are unfamiliar with the stages.

Whether you have looked at two pastors or fifty, you will be basing your decisions on information collected up to that point. This evaluation process will continue up to the final vote on which pastor to call. You will pass over some pastors in this process, and the field will narrow. When pastors with whom you have corresponded are dropped from consideration, each should receive a letter as soon as possible. Some pastors will likewise choose to eliminate themselves from consideration.

Making Your Recommendation

After your evaluation is complete, you will need to recommend to your board which pastor or pastors to invite for final consideration. This recommendation will be based on which pastors the committee thinks will make the best match for your congregation and ministries.

You could recommend one candidate. Some search committees recommend that the board present two pastors from which the congregation may choose. There are cases when three pastors are offered to congregations, but this option can be confusing to the parishioners. The committee members must be aware of denominational or regional rules that affect their decision.

If you have five pastors at the final stage, your choices should be based on your combined knowledge of all the information received and the results of your evaluation process. The committee's presentation to the board should focus on the committee's reasons for selecting a particular candidate and how he or she will meet the identified needs of the church. If you have kept the board members informed about your process and about the pastors you are considering, they will most likely concur. Once the recommendation is approved, move to chapter 12, "Managing the Call Process."

Nontraditional Recommendations

This section deals with calling seminary candidates, pastors from another denomination, and pastors for a specific term. Consult your denomination to determine if there are specific actions to consider. If you are not affiliated with a denomination, the information is still useful in understanding protocol for these situations.

Calling Seminary Candidates

Seminary candidates who have met the course and field requirements are often eligible for call after the appropriate seminary or denominational bodies have approved them. Their candidacy is often announced in a designated denominational medium. These candidates are typically treated the same as other pastors. Candidates who have trained in theological seminaries other than those approved by your denomination must usually meet specific denominational requirements. Investigate whether your denomination has guidelines for considering and calling these seminary candidates.

In some denominations, names of all pastors and seminarians eligible for call are made available through judicatory channels. But in other denominations, names of seminary candidates are available through the seminaries. If you wish to consider a student, contact the seminary of your choice in winter for names of students graduating at the end of the current or upcoming school year. Usually a specific individual or office at the seminary is responsible for placement.

Calling Pastors of Other Denominations

In the course of the search process, you may receive an inquiry from or know of a pastor who interests you but who is ordained in another denomination. If his pastoral profile interests you and you want to move him into your search process, you must consider the constraints placed upon you by your denomination. These cases must be managed with special care and attention to detail. Consult your denominational or regional offices for their assistance.

Initially you will work with a pastor from another denomination the same way you would work with a pastor of your own denomination. As you move further along in the process, however, you will have several additional tasks. First, your church order may contain special procedures to be followed if you decide to issue a call to him. Second, contact his local judicatory to determine if there were any problems in previous congregations. This last task should determine whether the candidate has a history of problems. Ask the hard questions. Such situations are rare, but occasionally a pastor will want to change denominations to leave behind a troubled history.

Some denominations will allow a pastor to be considered from another church body or tradition only after the congregation has put forth a sustained effort to find a minister from within the denomination. Two other situations may allow for approaching such a pastor.

◆ The minister to be called has such extraordinary qualifications that it is important for the denomination to acquire his or her services.

◆ The need of a particular congregation for a pastor is so urgent or the congregation's circumstances are so unusual that they can be met only by calling a minister from another denomination. This seems to happen most commonly when the church seeks an ethnic-minority pastor and the denomination has a shortage of such clergy, and in isolated rural areas where few pastors choose to serve and churches find that they must work across denominational lines to survive.

If you are considering a pastor from another denomination, contact your regional or denominational offices to determine what documentation they need to accept the pastor. You may need copies of his completed minister's profile form, academic degrees, seminary transcript, and ministry references. He may also be required to submit a statement attesting to his knowledge of your denomination's history, church order, and agencies and institutions. These are things the board can help the pastor learn.

Calling for a Specific Term of Service

On occasion, a church may desire to extend a call to a pastor for a specific term of service. The ministry may be new and have an uncertain future, or it may be funded for a specific length of time, or your congregation may be addressing a unique ministry opportunity with a limited time frame. In such situations, several procedures should be followed. First, be certain that your advertising and communications clearly state the length of the call. Second, the letter of call should designate the specific term, address the possibility and method for continuation of service (if applicable), and outline the financial arrangements if the call is not extended beyond the specified term. Third, your church counselor should determine that the termination procedures and arrangements in your letter of call are fair and reasonable.

It takes time to agree on the criteria you will use in evaluating pastors, and then to evaluate each pastor and determine how well he or she might fit your congregation. Finding the best match for your church and your ministries is vital. Spend time in prayer and lean on God

CHART 10.2. Task Cluster: Selection Criteria

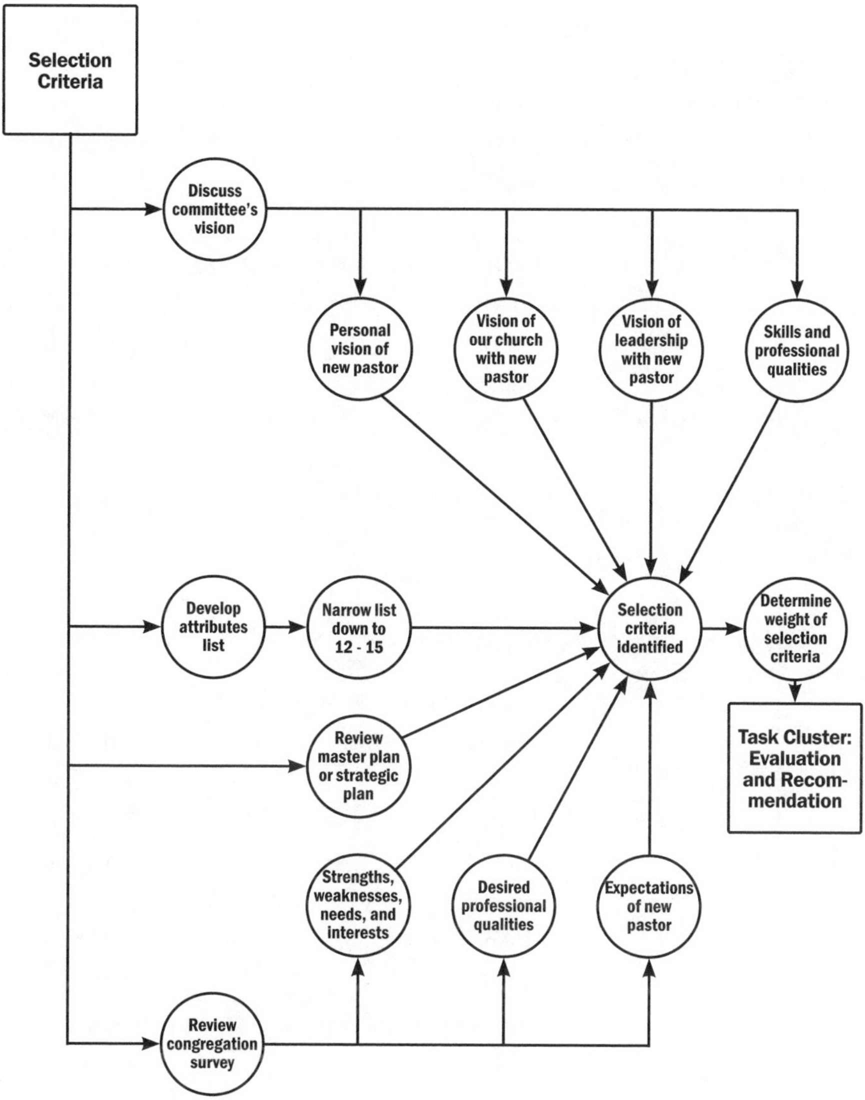

in this phase of the search. God will lead you to a recommendation. Once a pastor has been chosen, talk about the best way to present your congregation to the pastor and the pastor to the congregation.

CHART 10.3. Task Cluster: Evaluation and Recommendation

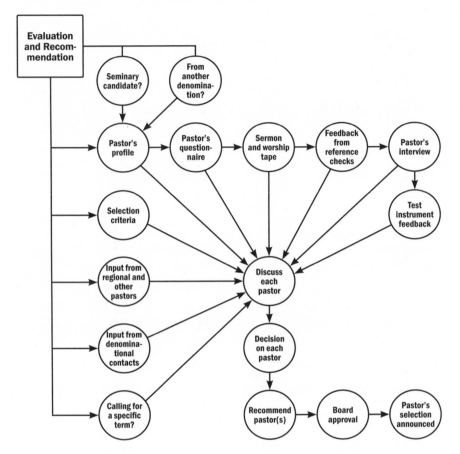

Chapter 11

Presenting Your Best Side

The materials you send a candidate about your congregation and the way you present yourself in hosting pastors create an impression in the pastor's mind. The candidate is forming opinions of how capable the leaders are, how friendly the congregation is, and whether the information you gave about your church is accurate. These impressions and opinions are an important part of the pastor's decision-making process. Surveyed pastors were clear on what influenced their decisions. Consider the following comments as you think about how to present your best side:

- ◆ "The primary factors were their clear vision, openness to change, and ongoing outreach."
- ◆ "Spend time with the board when visiting the church. Many churches tend to put 'forward-looking' people on the search committee and 'safe' people on the board. This results in tension when you arrive and find the actual picture different from what was presented."
- ◆ "Most important, they indicated that as a church they were willing to learn and follow my leadership."
- ◆ "They passionately pursued calling me, mobilizing the members to encourage me."
- ◆ "They let us know how they felt our gifts for ministry could be used."

♦ "Every church puts its best foot forward, but there are also the less involved and fringe members. Perhaps more opportunity should be given to talk to a wider cross-section of the church."

Hosting the Visit

Once a recommendation about which pastor to consider has been made and approved by the board, possible dates for a visit can be discussed with the candidate. You need to plan what will be done and with whom. The search committee can decide the order of activities on the basis of time available. If the pastor is married, his or her spouse should be included in the visit. Put together a visit that will hold the interest of the pastor and spouse and yet not be too tiring. Ask the pastor whether he would prefer to stay in a motel or with a host family. The value of fellowship and the beginning of friendships established through staying in a member's home cannot be underestimated. Be sensitive, however, to the fact that the interview process can be draining, and some pastors may prefer the privacy and emotional space afforded by a motel. The chance to take a break may allow the pastor to feel fresh and focused during the interview, the worship service, and social events. If you do use a motel, chose an upscale one. Below is a sample section from a letter with an agenda for a visit.

♦ ♦ ♦

Our tentative agenda for your visit here is listed below. This schedule is not cast in concrete, but we hope it will serve to provide an opportunity for us to get to know one another.

FRIDAY, JANUARY 8

8:00 PM Arrive at Anytown airport. The search committee chair and another committee member will pick you up and drive you to your host family.

SATURDAY, JANUARY 9

9:00 AM Breakfast meeting with board
10:30 AM Meeting with staff

12:00 noon. Lunch with interim pastor, search committee chair, and
    board president

2:00 PM Tour of the city

3:30 PM Free time

6:00 PM Potluck with search committee, board members, staff, and
    church committee leaders

SUNDAY, JANUARY 10

9:45 AM Sunday school. Let us know if you would like to teach a class
    or simply attend.

11:00 AM Morning worship service. Please let us know your sermon
    title and Scripture text.

12:15 PM Potluck and fellowship time

1:15 PM Question-and-answer time with the congregation

2:00 PM Meeting with members of search committee and board

5:00 PM Departure

Your airline tickets are enclosed. The weather here will likely be
cool—in the fifties. Please give me a call if you have any questions
or if you would like to suggest changes to the agenda and to discuss
the worship hour. We are truly looking forward to your time with us
and trust God to bless us all.

◆ ◆ ◆

When you invite each pastor and spouse in the call process to come
for a visit, make the visit fit the pastor and her family. It is important
for the search committee, board, staff, committee leaders, and their
spouses to spend time getting to know the pastor and her family. The
majority of the visit should be spent with these people. An evening
potluck can allow them time to talk with the pastor and spouse. One
person should facilitate the evening's event or social time. Allow time
for each person to share information about his or her ministry involvement in the church.

Encourage the pastor and her husband to ask any questions they
have about the church, its members and ministries. Ask the pastor if
she would like to know more about specific ministries or activities.

Have one individual work with the visiting pastor to plan the worship service. Whether through a deacon or elder, a worship leader, or the church secretary, the service needs to be coordinated with the pastor in advance of her arrival. Ask if she would like to offer a children's message. Let her know if the children are dismissed at a point in the service for children's church or Sunday school. Advise her of any elements in your worship service that you expect her to include; otherwise, the service should be hers to plan and lead, so that her gifts and ministry style come through. Let her know if you have PowerPoint or other media capabilities. Make her aware of any special worship ministries, such as choirs, praise teams, special instruments, drama, or puppets; and work with her to use one or two that fit with the message and flow of the service. Just as the service is for the congregation to be introduced to the pastor and to experience her leading worship, it should allow the pastor to see any exceptional worship elements your church has to offer.

Make each visit fit the makeup, interests, and needs of the pastor's family. If the pastor has children, allow time for the family to see area schools, and if possible, arrange for visits to tour the schools. Members of the congregation with school-age children might be asked to assist. If the church does not own a parsonage and the pastor may want to buy a home, be sure to show several neighborhoods in the area and to provide real estate ads from the local newspaper or appropriate websites.

Introducing Pastors to the Congregation

How you introduce the pastors to the congregation is important. The sample letter "Introducing Two Candidates to the Congregation" in appendix E shows an effective method of introducing two pastors to the congregation and conducting the voting process. Prepare a page about each of the pastors being presented for consideration, drawing from the pastoral questionnaire shown in appendix D. You may wish to summarize key questions and answers from the pastor. Add a family picture with the spouse's name and the children's names and ages. This summary allows the congregation an opportunity to get to know a bit about the pastor and her family before they visit. These profiles should be distributed the week before each pastor visits. A cover letter and the profiles should be mailed to all member households and put on the church's website. Additional copies can be put in the foyer for the day of the pastor's visit. If there are regional or denominational procedures for introducing candidates, follow them.

Talking about Expectations

While you are presenting your best side, hosting the pastoral candidates, getting to know them, and introducing them to your church and its ministries, and leaders, allow time to talk about any unanswered questions or expectations. During a face-to-face visit, new questions may surface. Through your analysis, self-study, and identification of styles and issues earlier in the search process, you took the first steps toward ensuring a good match with a new pastor. Now, as you meet face to face, you have the opportunity to clarify your expectations of a pastor and his or her expectations of your board and congregation. These expectations may concern ministry styles, leadership style, levels of involvement in church functions, vision, or worship style. If your church has strong convictions on specific issues, such as women holding elected office, it would be best for all concerned if these are addressed in early communications. If they have not been discussed earlier, however, they need to be discussed now. Your willingness to be candid with pastoral candidates can help avert problems that could later lead to pastor-church conflicts.

Little Things Make a Difference

Taking care of some basic courtesies can make a good impression. If air travel is necessary, you should be governed by the pastor's schedule and needs, and buy the airline tickets and send the itinerary and confirmation information to him or her. At least one search committee member should meet the pastor and spouse at the airport. You should plan on picking up all expenses related to the visits. When telephone calls are necessary, you should make the call and incur the expense. Take an area map and mark the homes of member families (or as many as possible), the church, and schools. A map gives a useful overview of the area.

Presenting yourself in the best light also means looking at the church facilities and the parsonage. When the search process begins, another group might be formed to do maintenance work that has been put off in the church and the parsonage. They need to look attractive.

Building a Compensation Package

The search committee, with the board or the finance committee, needs to develop a compensation package. While search committee members may not be actively involved in this work, they need to be certain the package is developed and ready for final approval once they have a decision on which pastor will be issued a call. The details need not be shared during the pastor's visit. General figures are adequate at this time.

Review any relevant denominational or regional compensation guidelines before developing your compensation package. These may address salary, components of an annual salary, a suggested base salary, benefits, and moving expenses. There may be allowances based on the size of the congregation, the job description, experience, and education. Ask how much leeway you have in building your compensation package.

Compensation can include any of the following: salary, vacation, defined days off, Social Security offset, housing (parsonage or a housing allowance), utility allowance, Christian school allowance for children, pension fund contributions, health insurance (this can include health, dental, and vision coverage), professional books and subscriptions allowance, educational allowance, entertainment allowance, auto allowance for business use of the pastor's personal vehicle, holidays, sick leave, maternity/paternity leave, worker's compensation, and sabbatical time. You should cover moving expenses. Candidates with furniture and the number of books most pastors have acquired could scarcely afford to accept a call if they had to pay for the move. Determine ahead of time what information about the compensation package will be presented to the congregation. It is easier to present an aggregate amount rather than to break it down item by item. Otherwise, list it as salary, benefits, and ministry allowances. Items like books and subscriptions, entertainment, and auto are not take-home pay but allowances for ministry-related expenses.

You may be totally on your own in creating and presenting your compensation package. Appendix F, "Sample Addendum to the Letter of Call," presents a sample package. Identified in detail are workdays, holidays and vacation, compensation, allowances, benefits, reimbursables, and additional agreements. You may believe that this document is too specific, but it is much better to put things in writing than to deal with issues later. Attention to detail before the call can help prevent future problems. Your package does not have to be as detailed but should reflect standards for your area, benefits your church can afford, and allowances adequate for the pastor's profession. Individuals working on the compensation package might call neighboring churches to determine customary ranges. Use these as guidelines in determining dollar amounts appropriate for your church.

Once the basic compensation package is ready, several decisions need to be made. First, decide whether you need to design several specific packages based on the pastors who may be called. If you anticipate presenting two candidates, you may need one package for each pastor, reflecting their respective experience and education levels. Second, determine whether you will make allowances for negotiations in the terms of the package. There may be a request from the pastor to change the amount of time or money designated for continuing education, to allow for a sabbatical after a certain number of years, or to change other components. A good resource for determining a fair compensation package is available from *ChurchLawToday.com*. The organization's *Compensation Handbook for Church Staff* is updated annually and is a comprehensive, ecumenical survey of ordained and nonordained staff. Click on the "Bookstore" button at the website to find the book.

The Issue of Pastoral Housing

Another area to discuss is pastoral housing. If the church owns a parsonage, state that fact in your church information packet. Of course, you hope the parsonage will meet the needs of the pastor's family. After the pastor and spouse have seen the parsonage, sit down and discuss any improvements, whether as simple as painting and wallpapering or as complex as installing new carpet and upgrading the kitchen. Expecting the pastor to live in a substandard home, especially if the rest of the congregation resides in more elegant dwellings, is unrealistic.

If you have a small parsonage and the pastor has a large family, you will need to discuss your options. Will the church consider buying a larger parsonage or adding on to the existing one? Will you rent out the existing parsonage and purchase another one for the pastor? What you are able to do may influence a pastor's decision.

Many pastors would prefer to own a home. This possibility may hinge on whether the pastor has built up equity from owning a home at a previous church. If the pastor will have the option of buying a home, let him know that you will help him find a reputable real-estate agent. If the pastor has school-age children, show the neighborhoods around the better schools. Whatever the option, do your best to help him have everything ready before his family has to move. Having to rent for a short period and then move again is a hardship on him and his family. If the pastor will live in the parsonage, consider giving him an equity allowance—a plan whereby he shares in the ownership of the home.

If necessary, establish a task force to investigate the options. Several possible arrangements are listed below. If you choose any arrangement other than the pastor's living in the parsonage or the pastor's buying a home without help from the congregation, be sure to have the church's legal counsel draw up an agreement that is fair to both parties. The housing market may change negatively, or the pastor may leave sooner than expected; the agreement protects involved parties. With all options, clarify the responsibilities of each party, dates when payments are due, and conditions placed on either party:

- ◆ The pastor makes the down payment and all other payments and owns the house. The church pays the pastor a monthly housing allowance.
- ◆ The congregation gives the pastor a loan to apply to the down payment. This loan could be interest-free or low-interest—payable on a specific date, when he purchases another home, or when he leaves the congregation.
- ◆ The congregation allows the pastor to purchase the parsonage from the church.
- ◆ The congregation creates an equity-share arrangement (for the parsonage or another home) with the pastor and the church, with each putting in a predetermined amount and each having a percentage at risk.

In the examples above, the pastor is still paid a housing allowance, but she is typically responsible for the maintenance, taxes, and insurance on the home. The pastor has to be able to document for the IRS that the allowance was used for mortgage or rent, utilities, maintenance, furnishings, and other expenses. In an equity-share arrangement, the church could be responsible for a percentage of maintenance costs above a predetermined amount that is agreed on by the pastor and the board. In all the options, the board needs to offer the pastor a fair housing allowance.

If you have a parsonage, work out the details of how maintenance will be managed. Is there an amount allotted in the budget for maintenance? Who is responsible for the work? What is the pastor responsible for? If utilities are paid by the congregation, determine which are covered: garbage, electricity, gas, basic land-line telephone including long distance, and water? How about a cell phone, cable TV, or Internet service? While these may seem to be simple questions, they can easily be overlooked and become problems later.

Presenting your best side is important. When pastors come to visit your church, they will watch closely how you present your church, its ministries, and the congregation. The congregation will be watching the pastors to see whether they are everything you said they were. A good presentation will help make the pastors' visits positive and exciting.

CHART 11.1. Task Cluster: Presenting Your Best Side

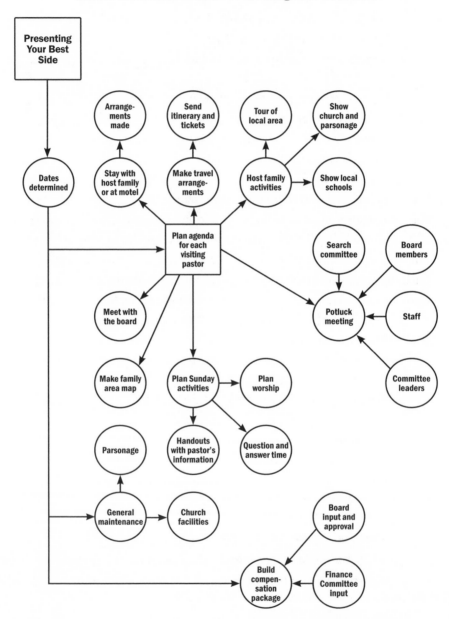

Chapter 12

◆ ◆ ◆

Managing
the Call Process

If your church is part of a denomination, you need to know what your church order or other guidelines say about calling a pastor. The guidelines may leave room for local options, or they may spell out rules to follow. Do not move forward in the call process without a thorough understanding of these requirements. If your church is independent, find out what your constitution and bylaws say, if anything, about the call process. If nothing is spelled out, you are free to proceed as the search committee and the board choose.

Guidelines typically address nominations, voting, and the role of denominational or judicatory staff. They might include:
- ◆ Number of people who must be nominated.
- ◆ Number of candidates the search committee shall recommend to the board.
- ◆ At what point in the deliberations candidates are invited to lead worship and preach to the full congregation.
- ◆ Who may vote.
- ◆ The margin by which a candidate must be approved (such as a simple majority or a two-thirds majority).
- ◆ Who makes the final decision (may be dictated by the church's constitution and bylaws).
- ◆ Steps that must be taken, perhaps involving judicatory staff, before the formal letter of call can be issued.

Options for Voting and the Call Process

Once the pastoral field has been narrowed to the best three to five candidates, the search committee needs to consider what method it will use when deciding which pastor to recommend or call, unless the procedure is laid out in your congregation's constitution and bylaws.

Some search committees, with their board's support, may feel comfortable selecting one candidate to present to the congregation. Congregational practice might even specify that the committee recommend only one candidate. Since the search committee members theoretically know more about the pastors and the congregation than anyone else, they are in the best position to judge the choices and to recommend one pastor. Talk this over as a committee, and if you decide to recommend one pastor, present your case to the board and ask for its approval. If the board was expecting two candidates, be prepared to defend your selection of one candidate.

Other search committees will present either two or three pastors. It is easier logistically to present two pastors than three. Two pastoral candidates can be invited to lead worship, preach, and meet with various groups on consecutive Sundays. With two pastors, both Sunday worship services will remain fresh in people's minds. Introducing three candidates over three Sundays makes it harder for people to remember which pastor they favor and for what reasons. Three candidates also tend to split the vote, making it more difficult for one to receive a wholehearted endorsement by the majority. Choosing between two pastors is difficult enough without introducing a third pastor into the equation.

Once a slate of candidates has been chosen, the board should manage the voting process, unless the congregation's constitution and bylaws specify otherwise. Again, there are several options, all presented below as if two pastors were being introduced. Whatever the decision, the board is probably charged with overseeing the voting process:

◆ The board presents the candidates to the congregation. The congregation meets and votes. The board then affirms the congregation's decision.

- ◆ The search committee presents the candidates to the board. The board votes, and the congregation is asked to affirm the board's decision.
- ◆ The search committee votes, the board affirms its work, and the congregation affirms the decisions of both the search committee and the board.

Designing Your Call Letter

Your letter of call should identify the work the pastor is being called to do and her compensation. Is her role clearly defined? Is compensation a part of the letter? Denominational or judicatory guidelines often speak to the content of the letter of call or how the letter is to be managed.

You have several options in writing your letter of call. If your denomination has an official letter of call, review it to determine whether it fits your needs and style. You may be required to use the official call letter, or it may be provided as a guide and you may be free to modify it. If you modify the letter, adhere to the basic intent. Any changes to the letter may have to be approved through your judicatory.

The letter of call should be signed by the board chair. Some churches will also have the secretary of the board sign the letter. Depending on denominational protocol, it may also need to be signed by your judicatory representative. Prepare the letter of call before the vote to call the pastor, and have it preapproved and signed by your counselor. If you are presenting two pastors for a vote, make a call letter for each pastor and have both letters signed by the counselor or supervisor, if required. Either of these letters will then be ready to be sent as soon as the call is approved. Consider including a cover letter signed by members of the search committee. A sample cover letter is provided in appendix G; a "Sample Letter of Call," which defines the call to the pastor, in appendix H; and a "Sample Addendum to the Letter of Call," which describes the compensation package, in appendix F. Together, these documents present a complete call package.

The Congregational Meeting

The congregational meeting to approve the call should be a formal business meeting. The recommendation from the search committee or board is presented, discussed, and put to a vote. Determine and publicize before the meeting who will be able to vote. Some denominations allow all confessing members to vote, while friends and constituents who attend the congregation's worship services regularly but who have not been baptized, confirmed, and added to the official membership rolls are not considered voting members.

Also determine and publicize what percentage of the congregation is required to vote in favor of a candidate in order for that person to be called as your next pastor. Some guidelines indicate that a call can be based on a simple majority; others require a two-thirds majority. Often after a vote is taken, the board will ask for a unanimous vote from the congregation. This second vote will then show the pastor that the full congregation is behind the call. This unanimous vote can be noted in the letter of call.

Depending on your guidelines, the board may need to meet to approve the congregation's decision. In some denominations, the vote by the congregation is advisory to the board, and the board may or may not choose not to issue the call as the congregation voted. If the board does not accept the voice of the congregation, the board members need to meet with the search committee to talk about their decision and then inform the congregation, giving their rationale. In all cases, the congregation needs to be reminded of the need to seek the will of God for the church.

Celebrating the Call

An alternative to the formal congregational meeting is to call together all members and friends of the congregation to affirm the decision within the context of worship. Come together to pray and worship with Scripture and song, announce the candidate, lead the congregation in small group prayers, and then ask for a vote of affirmation.

Close with praise songs and prayer. The sample service below can be modified to include your congregation's favorite songs and Scripture.

◆ ◆ ◆

CONGREGATIONAL PRAYER AND WORSHIP

Gathering Songs

"Seek Ye First the Kingdom of God"

"Spirit Song"

"With All My Heart"

"Change My Heart, Oh Lord"

Announcement of Candidate

"Open My Eyes, Oh Lord"

Prayer Sessions

Opening Prayer

Praise Prayers (Ps. 95:1–7)

Confession Prayers (1 John 1:6 and Isa. 59:2)

Thanksgiving Prayers (1 Chron. 16:8 and Ps. 105:5)

Intercession Prayers (Phil. 4:6–7 and Luke 18:1)

The Lord's Prayer

"Surely the Presence"

"In Your Time"

Vote of Affirmation

"Unto Thee, Oh Lord"

"Lord, Listen to Your Children Praying"

Closing Prayer

◆ ◆ ◆

Once the decision is made, several things need to happen. First, the search committee chair should call the chosen pastor and share the enthusiasm of the search committee, the board, and the congregation. Explain that a formal letter of call will follow (preferably by overnight mail or courier service). Second, telephone calls should be made to any other pastors who were considered. Third, if your church judicatory leader has not been personally involved in the voters' meeting, call him or her. Fourth, prepare the letter of call, if it was not written before the meeting. Make two copies, one for your records and one to be sent to the pastor. The board secretary should retain a copy of the board's letter for the church's minutes.

Generally, allow at least three weeks, or whatever time is specified in the guidelines you are using, for a response. You might also talk with the pastor to settle on an appropriate length of time for his decision. The pastor may request an extension. The search committee chair and committee, as well as the board, should keep in close contact with the pastor. You do not want to be pushy, yet you do want to be available to answer any questions. Do not give the pastor's contact information to the congregation. Respect the pastor's privacy and need for time to reflect, pray, and discuss the call with his family. Remember that some pastors may be considering two calls at one time. They may also be at different stages of an inquiry process with other churches.

Prayer Vigils and Prayer Cards

From the start of the search process, the congregation has been praying. Now that the members have chosen the pastor to be called, they need to be in focused prayer for that pastor. Make a poster on which members may sign up to pray in half-hour segments until an answer is received. They should pray for the pastor and her family and their decision. Place the poster in the foyer of the church and encourage people to sign up for a time period between 6:00 AM to 10:00 PM. Let the pastor know that the members are praying for her during this specific period. You may also post news on the church's website so that members are aware of the call.

Another idea is for the search committee to make tent cards that fold in the middle and have the same text on both sides. Members may put these on their tables and on their desks at work. These prayer cards can be a helpful reminder to pray for the pastor and her family as they consider the call. A sample prayer card is included on the next page.

Pray for Our Pastoral Call
Al Sayes
Pray for guidance
Pray for God's will for the Sayes family
Pray for Anytown Community Church
Al and Pat Sayes
Jamie (14), Jimmy (10), Jeffrey (8)
Cards or letters may be sent to
8765 Lively Road
Orange, CA 92866

When the Answer Is Yes

When the pastor's response is positive, the happy news should be spread quickly. Many members have been in constant prayer for a positive response, and they must be informed of the decision. Celebrate with the congregation.

If your denomination has rules about how to inform the congregation of the acceptance, follow them. Some denominations require posting the new pastor's name for several weeks in case there are objections from the congregation. If you have such constraints, respect them.

The acceptance phone call or letter may come to the president of the board or the chair of the search committee. Whoever receives the information should first call those who have dedicated themselves to constant prayer for the pastor and congregation, then the members of the search committee and the board. The easiest method of getting the word out, if the congregation is small, is to have the search committee, board members, or elders call the members. Letters can be sent to all members. Another method is to use a church e-mail list—but keep in mind that not everyone checks e-mail daily, or even uses e-mail. If you post the news on your website and then make phone calls, you can refer people to the website for further information. Your counselor or minister supervisor should also be notified.

The positive response is an affirmation of the life and value of the congregation. If a letter from the pastor has been received, read it to the congregation in the next worship service. Give thanks to God for his work in your search efforts. Have a time of praise and prayer. When the letter of acceptance comes, post it for the congregation to see. Encourage the congregation to send the pastor letters and cards that express their joy.

Maintain active communications until the pastor arrives. Ask the pastor whether he would like to receive materials via regular mail or e-mail, and make sure he has the URL of the church's website. The church secretary should begin sending him copies of your worship bulletins and newsletters. If the pastor has children, the Sunday school kids or the youth group can make a video to welcome any children in their age group. The secretary of the board can send copies of the board minutes and committee reports, so that the pastor will be aware of what is happening in the church. All these communications help the new pastor connect with his new church home. Consider writing a letter to his former church's board after your new pastor arrives, letting its members know you are praying for them.

When the Answer Is No

For many months, all of your energy was spent in the search process and then in issuing a call to your chosen pastor. Now you have received an answer: "No." As difficult as it may seem, you will need to pick up the pieces and regain the momentum you had before the call was declined.

The pastor's decision to decline the call will be hard for the search committee, since its members probably developed a close relationship with the candidate. Take time in your next meeting to talk about your feelings. Express your discouragement, and then move forward. Spend time in prayer. Even though you may be discouraged, remember to praise God for his hand in this conclusion to this phase of your search and trust that the decision was his will.

Rejections are hard to accept. One way of dealing with the negative response is to talk with the pastor and ask what factors influenced the decision to decline your call. Use the "No" as an opportunity to learn. Is there something in your presentation that needs improving? Did the pastor pick up on underlying issues in the congregation that need to be resolved? Was there a sense that you really do not know who you are or where you are going as a congregation?

It is easy to take a decision to decline a call personally, when in fact it is most likely due to a pastor's judgment that her ministry gifts do not match your vision or the ministry strengths and weaknesses of your congregation. This perspective can help you maintain a proper focus.

In reality, you will not be starting from scratch. If you presented two or three pastors to choose from, you will need to consider whether one of the other pastors will be your next choice. Do not automatically exclude them. One of these may be the right pastor. Some pastors will not entertain a call from a church if they know they were not the search committee's first choice, but others will. The committee needs to talk about it and decide whether to extend a call to one of them, since you have already interviewed them, invited them to visit, and talked in depth with them. How did the congregation receive them? Were their worship styles a good match? Dedicate yourselves to a time of prayer about this decision.

You also have a list of other pastors with whom you were working. Focus on this list, and consider bringing those candidates further along in the process. Some pastors who declined interest earlier may have indicated openness to hearing from you further down the road. Now may be the time.

Call your regional or denominational offices and request more names. Talk to contacts who have previously given you names. Consider calling pastors who have seen your church packet but who were not interested. Ask them about possible people to contact, or even if they themselves might now be interested.

This is a time to stay focused. You have a wealth of information about other pastors with whom you have been working. And there are still pastors to discover. One of these is the pastor God has chosen for your church.

If you received a no, you will continue your search efforts. If you received a yes, the board will take over to manage a smooth transition in leadership.

CHART 12.1. Task Cluster: Managing the Call Process

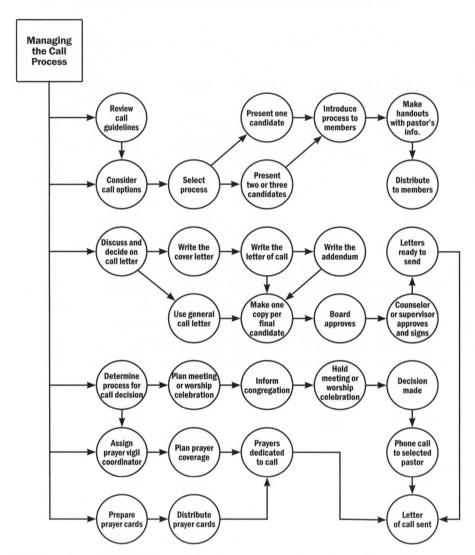

Chapter 13

◆ ◆ ◆

Managing a Smooth Transition

The search committee has a few details to wrap up before disbanding. Outstanding bills need to be paid and a final report made to the board. Letters need to be sent to any pastors who were still involved in any stage of the search, informing them of the acceptance of the pastor called by the congregation. Be sure to return any audio- or videotapes, CDs or DVDs, photographs, or other materials you received from these pastors. A sample letter follows:

◆ ◆ ◆

Dear Pastor Carol,

Our search has ended, and it was with excitement this past week that we received an acceptance from the Rev. Al Sayes to be our next pastor.

We thank you for being a part of our search. Our decision was a difficult one. The search committee has a warm spot in our hearts for you, for Tim, and for your ministry. We appreciate the honesty and genuineness that you conveyed in all our communications. As we struggled to find God's will for our church, we sought his guidance in prayer. Although our call was issued to Pastor Al, we were greatly impressed with your gifts for ministry and know that God has a special place for you with a congregation that will benefit from your warm and caring touch. We believe that God has led us to Pastor Al at this point in our congregation's life.

Our prayer for you is that you and your family will allow God to lead you into a new ministry or to a recommitment in your current ministry that fully employs your gifts for ministry.

If we can provide a reference or perspective to another search committee about you and your gifts for ministry, please let me know. We would be happy to assist you.

◆ ◆ ◆

The search committee members may decide to go out to dinner together to celebrate the positive conclusion of their efforts. Celebrate God's guidance in your search.

Making the Transition to Your New Pastor

When the call is accepted and announced to the congregation, the search committee members will phase themselves out of the picture. You have completed your assignment. Now the board needs to take charge and manage the transition.

If your church is small, a few members of the board might easily manage the arrival of your new pastor. Larger churches could establish a more formal transition team. With selected members of the board and search committee, and one or two staff members, the team could effectively manage the changes.

Once the call is accepted, the new pastor and the board will decide on a start date. This will be determined in part by the date when his current church will release him. Children's school terms, a spouse's job constraints, the sale of a home, or the desire for a vacation between assignments may also affect the starting date.

The interim pastor should be involved in the transition process, since he will be ending the special relationship he has had with the congregation. In the absence of an interim pastor, guest pastors need to be coordinated until the new pastor arrives. An installation date and service must be planned.

The board should prepare to help the new pastor make the transition into the life of the board, staff, committees, congregation, and community. Ask the pastor and spouse what information they need as they plan their move. They might appreciate help with moving, finding employment for the spouse, making school arrangements for their children, finding housing (if a parsonage is not available), continuing the pastor's benefits, and handling credentials and membership papers. Provide the names and telephone numbers of area pastors to help him establish important contacts. Make a map that shows where all the church families live, and provide a complete set of area maps. If the pastor is coming ahead of his family, because of the children's school year or the spouse's job constraints, consider having church families host him for occasional dinners, and give him a shopping basket full of food for other meals. Check ahead about favorite foods and food allergies.

Work with the incoming pastor to create a flyer about him and his family. A single page with family photos and a bit about each family member can be helpful in introducing the pastor and his family to the congregation. Make the flyer available to members on your website, via e-mail, and at church services. Church office staff can offer to help with ordering the pastor's business cards and stationery.

Keep in mind that until your pastor moves, he is still a pastor somewhere else. Be realistic about your expectations. Ask about the best times to contact him.

Continuing Benefits

The pastor's insurance and pension coverage can often be continued from the previous church. Be sure to ask whether unusual circumstances may require you to pick up the insurance or pension payments before the actual start date. There may be situations in which a pastor is paying for his own insurance coverage or has had his coverage terminated.

Credentials and Membership Papers

Depending on denominational protocol, the incoming pastor will make the necessary calls to update her credentials at the denominational office or have them released and sent to your church or a regional office, whichever is appropriate. If the credentials are sent to a regional office, request a copy for your board. The pastor will normally also take steps to have the memberships of her family transferred to your church. Determine whether the secretary of the board or the pastor will notify the necessary regional or denominational offices of the ministry change and starting date, or follow whatever procedures are in place for your denomination.

The Installation Service

The board, the incoming pastor, and the worship leader (if different from the pastor) need to plan the installation service. Local pastors and members of their churches may be invited. You may choose to have a special service with a guest pastor, praise team or choir numbers, member involvement, and the laying on of hands by other pastors or the board. The service will be the official starting point of the pastor and congregation's life together. Make this a service of celebration. It should be a memorable day for the pastor, his family, and the church. Consider hosting a reception or meal after the service.

If there are regional or denominational guidelines for an installation service, respect them. The supervising minister or other regional representatives might participate in planning the service.

Retaining Information
for the Next Search Committee

Once the search committee has disbanded, several things need to happen. First, the search committee secretary or chair should assemble one set of materials (correspondence, ads, brochures, bulletin announcements, Web posts, installation service bulletin, etc.) for recordkeeping

CHART 13.1. Task Cluster: Managing a Smooth Transition

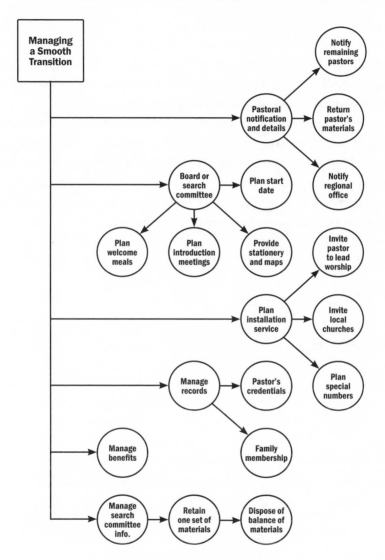

purposes. These should be stored in a secure location at the church. All pastoral profile forms should be destroyed. Some of the material used in a search can be helpful to the chair of the next search committee. One difficulty in forming an effective search committee is that, since searches tend to be infrequent, it can be hard to find people who have served before.

Second, committee members should properly dispose of their search materials and related papers and notes. It is best to collect their binders at a final committee meeting. The chair or secretary can manage disposal of the records. Paper shredders are commonplace and offer a practical way to dispose of paper records.

Once again, as a group, celebrate God's direction for your church. Many individuals have been blessed by their service on a pastoral search committee. You may be blessed with spiritual growth, a new awareness of the power of prayer, a deeper understanding of your church and its members and ministries, and a closeness to your new pastor. Celebrate God's gifts to the search committee and his gift of a new pastor for your church.

Appendix A

◆ ◆ ◆

Pastoral
Search Resources

Ministry Websites

◆ The Alban Institute *(alban.org)* offers resources for pastors and those interested in church life and development.

◆ Chrestone Consulting *(chrestoneonline.org)* is a Christian company that offers consulting, coaching, strategy planning, and much more.

◆ ChurchJobs *(churchjobs.net)* offers nationwide database searches of church and pastoral jobs.

◆ ChurchLawToday *(churchlawtoday.com)* is an extensive online legal library especially for churches and pastors. It includes preemployment screening services and resources on church finances, tax guidelines, and compensation; and it publishes an annual *Compensation Handbook for Church Staff.*

◆ ChurchStaffing *(churchstaffing.com)* is a source of information for churches and church staff members in personnel and staff relations.

◆ Congregational Resource Guide *(congregationalresources.org)* connects congregational leaders with resources that will enable them to face challenges and foster vitality in their communities of faith.

◆ Interim Ministry Network *(imnedu.org)*, an organization of professionals, is dedicated to the health and wellness of church congregations.

◆ Managing the Pastoral Search Process *(pastoralsearch.org)* is a resource created by the author to support this book.

◆ Ministry Staffing Search *(ministrystaffingsearch.org)* is a site where churches can post positions and pastors can post profiles. It includes a Ministry Compatibility Matrix service.

◆ MyChurch *(mychurch.org)* is a free online tool for churches to extend their communities between Sundays and to create an online community with personalized features.

◆ Pastor Search Network *(pastorsearch.net)* helps churches find pastors and ministerial staff.

◆ Orange Tree Employment Screening *(www.orangetreescreening.com)* specializes in working with churches.

◆ Oxford Document Management Company *(oxforddoc.com)* specializes in background checks for churches.

Internet Tools

◆ *Blogger.com* is a free hosted blogging service with easy-to-create templates and features.

◆ *Feedblitz.com* automates the process of turning blogs into feeds with subscription features.

◆ *Feedburner.com,* a Google offering, gives blogs "feed" capability, permitting instant distribution of content and the possibility of subscribing to the content's feed.

◆ *InstantSurvey.com* offers online survey software tools for creating surveys, sending e-mail invitations, and analyzing survey data. There are two levels of fee-based service.

◆ *LinkedIn.com* is an interconnected network of professionals with the ability to form a group on a particular subject. You can find, be introduced to, and collaborate with others through your profile and groups.

◆ *QuestionPro.com* provides online survey software tools for creating surveys, sending e-mail invitations, and analyzing survey data. It offers two levels of fee-based service.

◆ *Skype.com* enables free Skype-to-Skype video and voice calls through your computer.

◆ *SurveyMonkey.com,* a free, powerful web-based online survey service, enables anyone to create professional online surveys quickly and easily.

◆ *Typepad.com,* a hosted blog service that charges users a small fee, has a simple start-up process and many customizable features.

◆ *Wordpress.com* offers software that allows you to easily create a blog hosted by Wordpress.

◆ *Wordpress.org* is a free, open-source blogging tool that you can download, configure, and upload to your website host.

◆ *YouTube.com* is a free website where you can upload any video, so that anyone can view it.

◆ *Zoomerang.com* features online software tools for creating surveys, sending e-mail invitations, and analyzing survey data. It offers a free limited service and two levels of fee-based service.

Appendix B

◆ ◆ ◆

Sample Pastoral Roles, Responsibilities, and Relationships

Anytown Community Church Pastoral Roles, Responsibilities, and Relationships

Leadership

The pastor, with the deacons, is to provide spiritual leadership to the church. The pastor is called first to a ministry of preaching and teaching of the Word and administration of the sacraments, and second, to the equipping of the saints. Leadership in other areas must be based upon personal giftedness.

Authority

The pastor has the authority to lead the church. He or she is supported by the board, staff, and committee leaders. The Pastoral Relations Committee will address concerns regarding authority. Certain responsibilities and authorities have been delegated by the board to committees, as defined in the "Anytown Community Church Policy and Structure Manual"; therefore, that organizational structure must be respected and utilized by staff and volunteers to the fullest extent possible.

Commitment

The pastor must be committed to the vision and mission of Anytown Community Church and the ministries that flow from them. This commitment will be reflected in his or her service to the board and committees, the church membership, prayer, the ministries of Anytown Community Church, and continuing pastoral education.

Vision Development

The pastor will set the vision for the church, in cooperation with board. His or her giftedness and position allow sharper insight and a broader view than those of others. The pastor needs to allow board members their visions, and the board needs to allow the pastor his vision. Collectively, a single vision statement will be developed. Supporting goals and objectives will be developed or refined annually. These then will be presented the congregation for their support.

Personal Giftedness

Recognizing that each individual is uniquely gifted for ministry, the pastor may choose to delegate certain areas of his or her service to others and/or assume other areas of service. The Pastoral Relations Committee should affirm the pastor's ministries. Staff and committee leaders may also provide input. Reviews of the pastor's ministry areas will be done annually in conjunction with the pastoral evaluation.

Equipping and Enabling

The pastor will disciple and mentor key leaders and potential leaders within the church body. This may be done through teaching in specific areas such as gifts, administration, discipleship, prayer, and vision development, and may include attending seminars with board members or key leaders. Equipping and enabling leaders should be a ministry priority. Equipping and enabling of the general congregation should be done through sermons and Sunday school teaching.

Relationship to Staff

The pastor is ordinarily charged with the supervision of the staff unless otherwise decided by a joint decision between the pastor and the board. The hiring and termination of staff will be carried out in accordance with staff members' individual contracts and shall be reviewed by the Pastoral Relations Committee.

Relationship to Board

The pastor is ordinarily the president of the board. Cooperative leadership is expected from both the pastor and the board members. Each has the authority to hold the other accountable. Common submission to the will, wisdom, and vision of God for the church at this time, in this place, with God's people, is vital. Just as the board is to conduct an annual pastoral evaluation, so the pastor will conduct an annual evaluation of the board. The Pastoral Relations Committee will address any areas of concern.

Relationship to Committee Leaders

The pastor will work closely with the committee leaders. He or she, with the help of the Administration Committee, is responsible for equipping committee leaders to serve more effectively in their ministry roles.

Appendix C

◆ ◆ ◆

Sample Congregational Survey

Anytown Community Church Congregational Survey

The Pastoral Search Committee will use information from this survey in selecting a pastor. It will both assist in the evaluation of our unique needs as a congregation and give prospective pastors an insight into who we are. Because the search committee is trying to move quickly to develop a profile of our church, *we ask that you return this survey by 5:00 PM on Monday, August 14.* Please place completed surveys in the box on the table in the foyer or mail them to the church. We may not be able to incorporate into the church profile surveys returned at a later date.

We ask that each regularly attending teenager and adult complete a survey. Completed results will be posted. Individual responses are confidential. Your input is extremely important, and we thank you for your participation.

Name (optional) _____

Anytown Community Church Affiliation Information

Please circle your answers.

Anytown Community Church affiliation: Member   Nonmember

Length of time associated with Anytown Community Church:

less than 1 year   1-5 years   6-10 years   11-20 years   over 20 years

Personal Information

Please circle your answer.

Sex: Male   Female

Age range:

13-19   20-29   30-39   40-49   50-59   60-69   70 and over

Occupation:

Student   Homemaker   Professional Trades   Sales   Agriculture
Business   Retired   Other _____

Ethnic background:

Caucasian   African-American   Hispanic   Asian   American Indian
Other _____

Other than Sunday worship, do you participate in any ministries, programs, or activities of the church?   Yes   No

Do you participate in any outreach (i.e. evangelistic) ministries?   Yes   No

Desired Professional Skills of Our Next Pastor

Circle one for each topic: 1 = unimportant, 2 = important, 3 = very important

Preaching	1	2	3
Conducting worship	1	2	3
Teaching	1	2	3
Pastoral care	1	2	3
Counseling	1	2	3
Problem solving	1	2	3
Program development	1	2	3

Evangelism leadership	1	2	3
Ministering to elderly	1	2	3
Ministering to children and youth	1	2	3
Ministering to families	1	2	3
Church administration	1	2	3
Ministering to the sick	1	2	3
Conflict resolution	1	2	3
Community involvement	1	2	3
Cooperation with board	1	2	3
Setting vision & goals	1	2	3
Training leaders	1	2	3
Building committees	1	2	3

Expectations of Our Next Pastor

Rank the following list in numeric order, with 1 being the most important and 8 being the least important.

Makes it a priority to visit the church members _____

Is energetic and charismatic in worship _____

Focuses primarily on the worship service _____

Works with the board in setting visionary leadership _____

Helps us develop a strong outreach into the community _____

Helps us develop small groups _____

Helps us develop strong board and committee leaders _____

Helps us develop more programs for members and visitors _____

Strengths and Weaknesses of Our Congregation

Please evaluate the relative strength of our church in these ministry areas. Circle one for each topic: 1 = weakness, 2 = average, 3 = strength.

Evangelism	1	2	3
Discipleship	1	2	3
Community outreach	1	2	3
Global mission support	1	2	3
Doctrinal teaching	1	2	3

Managing conflict	1	2	3
Ministry to children	1	2	3
Ministry to youth	1	2	3
Ministry to singles	1	2	3
Ministry to families	1	2	3
Ministry to elderly	1	2	3
Ministry to women	1	2	3
Ministry to men	1	2	3
Ministry to seniors	1	2	3
Bible studies	1	2	3
Spiritual growth	1	2	3
Fellowship	1	2	3
Caring for the poor	1	2	3
Music ministry	1	2	3
Welcoming visitors	1	2	3
Liturgy	1	2	3
Worship services	1	2	3
Unity	1	2	3
Care giving	1	2	3
Shepherding	1	2	3
Faithfulness	1	2	3
Nurturing	1	2	3
Counseling services	1	2	3
Commitment	1	2	3
Stewardship	1	2	3
Denominational participation	1	2	3
Supporting families	1	2	3
Adult education	1	2	3
Sunday school	1	2	3
Administration	1	2	3
Vacation Bible School	1	2	3
Openness to change	1	2	3
Meeting goals	1	2	3
Cooperating with other churches	1	2	3
Defining our mission and & vision	1	2	3

Our Congregation

Circle one for each sentence: 1 = false, 2 = somewhat true, 3 = true.

Our members care about one another.	1	2	3
Our members volunteer readily for church activities.	1	2	3
Our members give generous financial support to the church.	1	2	3
Our congregation supports its committees.	1	2	3
Members with broken lives find a safe haven in our church.	1	2	3
Our congregation supports the board.	1	2	3
The board encourages members to use their talents in worship services.	1	2	3
The board sets worthy examples for the congregation.	1	2	3
Our congregation cooperated well with our previous pastor.	1	2	3
Our next pastor can count on the wholehearted cooperation of the congregation.	1	2	3

Please contact a member of the search committee if you have any questions regarding this survey.

Appendix D

Sample Pastoral Questionnaire

Anytown Community Church
Pastoral Questionnaire

Please write a few thoughts about each topic listed below. We are interested, for your sake and ours, in relevant and concise statements of your thoughts and feelings as these phrases relate to you and your ministry.

Personal Information

Name:_____ Year of ordination:_____

Home Phone: ( )_____ Office Phone: ( )_____

E-mail: _____ Fax: ( )_____

Spiritual gifts:

(1)_____ (2)_____ (3)_____

Spouse's name: _____

Does your spouse have a role in your ministry or in the church? If so, please describe.

_____

_____

Children:

(1) _____ Age _____ (2) _____ Age _____

(3) _____ Age _____ (4) _____ Age _____

(5) _____ Age _____

Do you own your own home?   Yes   No

Would you prefer to live in a parsonage _____ ? Or your own home _____ ?

Thoughts about ministry

The areas of ministry I find most challenging are:

_____

The areas of ministry I find most satisfying are:

_____

The areas in which I most need to grow are:

_____

Why are you open to a new call at this time?

_____

What would you like to find in making a church change?

_____

Describe your thoughts about leadership:

My style of leadership is:

_____

I hope my relationship to the board will be:

_____

I hope my relationship to staff and committee leaders will be:

_____

Developing and nurturing a vision means:

_____

Involving others in lay ministry means:

_____

I mentor others by:

_____

I foster commitment and accountability by:

_____

Describe your thoughts about administration

I think administration of the church's business is:

_____

The board and committees assist in the church's administration by:

_____

Describe your thoughts about worship

The worship style I prefer is:

_____

My preaching style is:

_____

Lay participation in worship should include:

_____

Describe your thoughts about education

Good children's and youth ministry includes:

_____

Family ministry means:

_____

Adult education is:

_____

Describe your thoughts about evangelism

Evangelism allows the church to:

_____

Training others for evangelism means:

_____

Evangelism is:

_____

Describe your thoughts about fellowship

Good church fellowship is:

_____

I think family visiting is:

_____

Caring for one another means:

_____

Please write any questions you have for us on another sheet of paper.

◆ ◆ ◆

Sample Letter Introducing Two Candidates to the Congregation

Anytown Community Church
Pastoral Search Committee

Dear Members of Anytown Community Church,

The Pastoral Search Committee requests and encourages full participation of the congregation in the next phase of the pastoral search process.

Before inviting pastoral candidates to Anytown Community Church to meet the congregation, the committee asked each candidate to provide extensive written, oral, and recorded material. The search committee has made every effort to match the skills and gifts of the candidates with the unique qualities and needs of Anytown Community Church.

We present two candidates at this time, believing fully that both are well suited and qualified for ministry with us. Attached are profiles of the Rev. Al Sayes, whom we will host on January 10, and the Rev. Carol Collins, who will be with us on January 17. Please review their profiles before their visits.

During the visits, the pastors and their spouses will have an opportunity to meet with the board, staff, and committee leaders. They will also tour the community and other points of interest. On Sunday the visiting pastor will lead us in our morning worship. After worship there will be a question-and-answer period for the congregation to converse directly with the candidate. A fellowship time will follow.

After both candidates have made their visits, each member of the congregation will have an opportunity to decide which candidate he or she believes is best suited for ministry here.

The information gained from this process, in addition to the prior research, will be considered by the search committee in determining which candidate to recommend to the board for a call. If the board endorses the candidate, the recommendation will be presented to the congregation for a vote of affirmation. A Congregational Prayer and Worship Celebration is scheduled for Sunday evening, January 24, at 6:30 PM for this vote.

During this phase of the process, we again ask for your fervent prayers for each of the candidates as well as the search committee, that we may all be receptive to the leading of the Holy Spirit. Ultimately we acknowledge that it is God who calls the man or woman and merely uses us as willing servants to accomplish this task.

If you have questions about the candidates or the process, please call any member of the search committee.

Sincerely,
Your Church Board and the Search Committee

Appendix F

◆ ◆ ◆

Sample Addendum to the Letter of Call

An Addendum to the Letter of Call from the Board of the Anytown Community Church to Pastor Al Sayes

Work and Leave

1. Your work not only includes ministry at the Anytown Community Church but may also include work in the community on behalf of the church. The pastor's scheduled workweek is five days, which shall include Sunday activities. The pastor is expected to preserve at least one 24-hour period each week solely for personal and family time.

2. You will have the following periods of leave at full compensation:

   a. _____ national holidays and _____ floating holidays to be taken so as not to interfere with worship for the major church seasons.

   b. _____ weeks of annual vacation consisting of _____ workdays, which shall include _____ Sundays. No more than _____ days and _____ Sundays may be carried over into the following year unless agreed upon in mutual consent with the board.

   c. _____ days of continuing education leave, including _____ Sundays, are granted each year.

Compensation

1. Salary, allowances, benefits, and reimbursables listed below will be paid monthly.
2. Your annual compensation, allowances, benefits, and reimbursables package will be reviewed by the board and adjusted annually.

Base Salary

Your annual base salary will be _____.

Allowances

The church shall pay the following allowances:
1. A Social Security offset allowance of _____.
2. The use of the parsonage, or a housing allowance in the amount of _____ annually.

Benefits

The church shall pay the following benefits:
1. Medical and dental insurance to provide full family coverage.
2. A term life insurance policy for the pastor in the amount of _____.
3. A pension contribution in the amount of _____ yearly.
4. School tuition assistance in the amount of _____ for any dependent(s) attending a Christian elementary school or high school, or full-time, four-year college.
5. Parsonage utilities (excepting personal long-distance calls).

Reimbursables

The church shall pay the following reimbursables as incurred in fulfilling the duties of your office:

1. Travel expenses, up to _____ yearly, paid at the mileage rate established by the IRS, plus out-of-pocket costs for parking fees and tolls, will be paid monthly.
2. Hospitality expenses, up to _____ yearly, will be reimbursed monthly for expenses occurred in the course of professional and social activities on behalf of Anytown Community Church.
3. Books, magazines, and other related professional materials expenses will be reimbursed monthly, up to _____ yearly, for materials necessary to maintain the pastor's library and resources.
4. Expenses for continuing education, up to _____ yearly. Upon mutual agreement, for specific continued education, _____ percent of this amount may be carried over to the next year.

Roles, Responsibilities, Relationships, and Support

1. "Pastoral Roles, Responsibilities, and Relationships" are described in the paper following this addendum. Described are areas of leadership, authority, commitment, vision casting, personal giftedness, equipping and enabling, and relationships to staff, board members, and committee leaders.
2. The Pastoral Relations Committee functions to aid in your spiritual and emotional well being.

Other Agreements

1. If you want to purchase a home, and finances of both parties allow, the board will negotiate with you for an acceptable housing allowance or equity share agreement.

2. All moving and travel expenses incurred in making your move to the Anytown area will be paid by the Anytown Community Church.

3. All pay and benefits shall become effective on _____ .

4. All compensation, allowances, benefits, vacation, and continuing education leave will be prorated for any partial years of service.

5. The letter of call and this addendum shall be made part of the minutes of the next Anytown Community Church board meeting following its signing by both parties.

_____   _____
Date   President of the Board

_____   _____
Date   Secretary of the Board

Concurrence:

_____   _____
Date   Pastor

Appendix G

◆ ◆ ◆

Sample Cover Letter for the Letter of Call

January 24, 2010

Dear Pastor Al,

It is with great excitement and anticipation that we sign this cover letter to our letter of call. We invite you to minister with us and to us in the Lord's work at Anytown Community Church.

You have touched our hearts, given warmth, and provided a sense of hope for what we can do together as God's church ministering to one another and seeking to minister more to our community. We believe that your gifts, ministry style, leadership skills, and personality can move us toward our vision and mission while keeping us focused on our core values.

We believe we can offer you a church family that will love you and care for you as an individual, as well as for your family. We commit to work side by side with you in the Lord's work, to serve under your leadership, and to be happy in the Lord with you.

The attached letter of call has been committed to the Lord. We trust in his guidance as you consider this call to ministry here with us. Our prayers will be with you and your family as you commit this decision to the Lord.

With his love and in his service,

Board Members   Pastoral Search Committee Members

_____   _____

_____   _____

_____   _____

_____   _____

_____   _____

_____   _____

_____   _____

_____   _____

_____   _____

_____   _____

Appendix H

◆ ◆ ◆

Sample Letter of Call

Anytown Community Church

January 24, 2010

Dear Pastor Al,

The Board of Anytown Community Church has the honor and pleasure to inform you that you have been chosen by a unanimous vote at a local congregational meeting held on January 24, 2010, to be our pastor.

On behalf of our congregation, we therefore extend to you this letter of call and pray that you will come and minister to us and with us.

The work we expect of you, should it please the Lord to send you to us, consists of preaching and teaching, leading the church and the board, family visiting and calling on the sick with the elders, and all things that pertain to the work of a faithful and diligent servant of the Lord, all in accord with the Word of God. The attached "Pastoral Roles, Responsibilities, and Relationships" further define these areas.

We know that the laborer is worthy of his hire. To encourage you in the discharge of your duties and to free you from material need while you are ministering and preaching and teaching God's Word to us, the board of Anytown Community Church promises to pay you a generous compensation package and allowances for benefits, and to reimburse you to offset expenses. These amounts are detailed in the addendum to this letter of call.

May our Lord impress this call upon your heart and give you guidance that you may arrive at a decision that is pleasing to him and, if possible, gratifying to us.

Yours in Christ,
The Board of Anytown Community Church of Anytown, Massachusetts

_____ , President of the Board
_____ , Secretary
_____ , Church Counselor

Bibliography

Achtemeier, Elizabeth. *So You're Looking for a New Preacher.* Grand Rapids: Eerdmans, 1991.

Berry, Erwin. *The Alban Personnel Handbook for Congregations.* Bethesda: Alban Institute, 1999.

Devore, Douglas E. *In Search of God's Man: A Help for Pulpit Committees.* Greenville, S.C.: BJU Press, 2002.

Geitz, Elizabeth Rankin. *Calling Clergy: A Spiritual and Practical Guide Through the Search Process.* Harrisburg, Pa.: Church Publishing, 2007.

Ketcham, Bunty. *So You're on the Search Committee,* revised edition. Herndon, Va.: Alban Institute, 2005.

Mead, Loren B. *A Change of Pastors . . . And How It Affects Change in the Congregation,* revised edition. Bethesda: Alban Institute, 2005.

Nicholson, Roger S. *Temporary Shepherds: A Congregational Handbook for Interim Ministry.* Bethesda: Alban Institute, 1998.

Oswald, Roy M., James M. Heath, and Ann W. Heath. *Beginning Ministry Together: The Alban Handbook for Clergy Transitions.* Bethesda: Alban Institute, 2003.

Umidi, Joseph L. *Confirming the Pastoral Call: A Guide to Matching Candidates and Congregations.* Grand Rapids: Kregel Academic & Professional, 2000.

Virkler, Henry A. *Choosing a New Pastor: The Complete Handbook.* Eugene, Ore: Wipf & Stock, 2006.

Williamson, Gerald. *Pastor Search Committee Planbook.* Nashville: B&H Publishing Group, 2000.

Withers, Robert. *Charting the Course: The Pastoral Search Process.* Raleigh, N.C.: *Lulu.com*, 2007.